T0157566

POLITICALLY UN-CORRECT

America's Crisis and Some Ways We Can Save Our Country

ROBERT ALAN

iUniverse, Inc.
Bloomington

Politically Correct
America's Crisis and Some Ways We Can Save Our Country

iUniverse books may be ordered through booksellers or by contacting:

iUniverse
1663 Liberty Drive
Bloomington, IN 47403
www.iuniverse.com
1-800-Authors (1-800-288-4677)

ISBN: 978-1-4697-9719-9 (sc)
ISBN: 978-1-4697-9720-5 (e)
ISBN: 978-1-4697-9721-2 (dj)

Printed in the United States of America

iUniverse rev. date: 5/3/2012

INTRODUCTION

The problem as I see it.

I hope and pray that as you read this politically un-correct book that you will become aware of the crisis' we are facing in America. I hope you will join me at the ballot box and start taking our country back from those who are destroying it, mostly the thieves and scalawags we have in our nation's capitol both elected and appointed...

For God's sake congress, stop pissing away money you don't have and that your bunch of thugs in the IRS can't collect. America is nearly $15 trillion dollars in debt and you are still spending all the taxes that you can collect and borrowing more money and spending that. *Stop it!!!*

If you, the American Voter, don't get involved, America will be a complete socialist state in one more generation and Americans will be a minority in what used to be their country.

The American People have been letting other people do their thinking for them. The media, with its "spin doctors" both print media and electronic media have been feeding the American Voters only what they want them to hear.

The American Voters have become apathetic and disgusted with our government. Our governments, Federal, State and local are stealing us blind! Their appetite for spending our tax money is totally out of control. When I hear our government leaders decry budget shortfalls, I never hear them "we have to cut spending" it's always "what new tax can we levy and what old taxes can we raise"? They voice loudly that they can't possibly cut the spending anymore. If they cut the budget, it's always some high profile vital public service that the public makes them restore and nothing ends up getting cut out of the budget.

As you read this book, I am going to continue to repeat over and over some of the things that I think are crucial to America surviving as our forefathers intended. I am going to repeat them over and over through several chapters in hopes that they will sink into the readers enough to get involved in saving our country.

I have already posted some of the contents of this book on the internet. I have included some of the wisdom and parts floating around on the internet for your review. I have included some of the wisdom passed on to me by some older men that I was around in my youth. Honesty, honor, integrity, friendship, and the love of America were some of the values that America was founded on.

Take heed, if you have not voted or have not been involved in selecting our country's leaders at the federal, state and local levels, you are BETRAYING America. If you do not involved soon it will be too late. America as our founding fathers envisioned it will be gone forever.

A nation of sheep breeds a pack of wolves.

TABLE OF CONTENTS

Chapter #1
The Debt Crisis and Obama's
Incompetence Personified

In my opinion, our current president is a liar and a fraud. He is a self professed Muslim. He had no experience to justify being president and I am still not satisfied with his place of birth or his undocumented background. Where are all his school records? How did he finance his education? Why is it, that most of his and his wife's' records are not available? What country issued him his first passport?

He made numerous promises during the campaign that he did not keep. The one I best remember was, "no earmarks will get past my desk". His 700+ billion "bail-out" was loaded with earmarks added by greedy congress folks who knew Obama had to pass them. Most of these "earmarks" had nothing to do with the bail-out and only added to the already high deficit. Obama has spent more money than all other presidents combined. America is now trillions of dollars in debt and congress is still spending.

Solving the Debt crisis had a simple solution that would have put America back on track. Instead of giving billions of dollars to undeserving companies that are largely responsible for this financial crisis, here is a plan floating around the internet from a Florida Newspaper that would have worked.

There are 40 million workers over the age of 50 in the work force. Pay them one million dollars each, with the following stipulation:

- They must retire. Forty million job openings un-employment fixed
- They must buy a new vehicle. Forty million vehicles ordered- auto industry fixed
- They must buy a house or pay off their mortgage – housing crisis fixed

The 400 Billion this program would have cost is less than the 780 Billion to bail out a bunch of thieves that had systematically looted the financial industry with exorbitant pay, bonuses, incompetent management and by defrauding their stock holders. The financial industry should have a mass of law enforcement people investigating them for fraud, deceitful practices, corruption, thievery. In my opinion a lot of the people that ran Wall Street into bankruptcy and financial problems, in my opinion, belong in prison right beside Bernie Madoff.

These folks that wrecked the financial industry should be held accountable civilly and have their assets stripped and given to the stockholders.

Now America is in a debt crisis as never before seen! This crisis did not occur recently, but has been building for years through several presidencies and the tenure of many career politicians (some with 30+ years in congress). The latest example of this crisis being created is to look at Obama's stimulation bill. There were billions of dollars or "earmarks" that had nothing to do with the badly needed help for the American worker. The stimulation paid a lot of obscene bonuses to a lot high dollar Wall Street political supporters and the only benefit of the "Cash for clunkers program" was that it got most of the

"Obama" bumper stickers off the road. It was a miserable failure financially.

The "CATO" Institute had more than 250 economic experts caution him that more government spending would not improve the economy. "To improve the economy, policy makers should focus on reforms that remove impediments to work, saving, investment and production. Lower tax rates and a reduction in the burden of government are the best ways of using fiscal policy to boost economic growth". (The Boston Globe February 9, 2009 page A5)

This stimulus was not the first time that numerous "earmarks" by members of congress have run up an obscene amount of spending with little or no public review or knowledge.

We have now gotten into two wars that we had or have no hope of winning, the congressional leaders and the presidents have lied to the American People about both of them. We are still fighting them at a cumulative cost of trillions of dollars and no end in sight. And civilian politicians have interfered with our military in a war the military is trying to win.

Obama spends $20M+ in tax payer dollars by executive order, to immigrate Hamas Refugees to the USA. This is the news that did not, and will not, make the headlines. Where the hell is the media on this issue? In a time of double digit un-employment, Obama imports Muslims that hate our county at American Taxpayers expense...

By executive order, President Barack Obama has ordered the expenditure of $20.3 million in "migration assistance" to the Palestinian refugees and "conflict victims" in Gaza" at a time when America has double digit unemployment and many American Families living at or below poverty level. We have homeless veterans living in their cars looking for a job and some of them needing medical help that they were promised. There are still children in America going to bed hungry every night and Obama has the balls to spend taxpayer's money on Palestinians.

The "presidential determination" (ain't that nice?) which allows hundreds of thousands of Palestinians with ties to Hamas to resettle in the United States, was signed and appears in the Federal Register.

Few on Capitol Hill, or in the media, took note that the order provides a free ticket replete with housing, transportation and food allowances to individuals who have displayed their overwhelming support to the Islamic Resistance Movement (Hamas) in the parliamentary election of January 2006. The American Taxpayers get screwed again.

Now we learn that he is allowing thousands of Palestinian refugees to move to, and live in, the US at American taxpayer expense. These are people that expressed hatred for the American way of life and are now coming to live in America at American Taxpayers expense.

These important, and insightful, issues are being "lost" in the blinding bail-outs and "stimulation" packages and being ignored by our irresponsible and biased media.

To verify this for yourself:

www.thefederalregister.com/d.p/2009-02-04-E9-2488

As I am finishing this book, Obama is traveling in airplanes at the taxpayer's expense trying to drum up support for his latest jobs fiasco and accusing the republicans of blocking it. The republicans are still wondering how he is going to fund all these jobs? Borrow some more money and increase the national debt some more? I find it a bit convenient that the funding for this vital and altruistic jobs bill runs just past the 2012 presidential election.

As I review Obama's efforts at creating jobs during his political career, I wonder about his "earmark" as a senator that funded a job for his wife at a Chicago Hospital? I wonder about the millions sent to an Oregon School where his brother-in-law is a basketball coach?

He is promising college graduates relief from their student loans. He is overlooking the point that a college education costs have risen to obscene levels. The cost of a college education today with college presidents demanding and getting multi-million dollar salaries is, in my opinion, bordering on criminal conduct. College tuition today has risen to ridiculous levels.

Obama has spent more money than all the preceding U.S. Presidents combined. America now has a multi-trillion national debt and Obama is advocating spending more borrowed money to fund "teachers, firefighters and policemen". In my opinion, these should be locally funded and are not the responsibility of the federal government.

When the 2012 presidential election approaches, keep in mind that, in my opinion, the liberal media has again chosen Obama as their "poster boy". In my opinion, the liberal media is going to do everything foul, immoral or biased to get Obama re-elected. Try to carefully evaluate their liberal media output and measure it carefully against other sources on media and what you know to be the truth.

Obama's Historic Firsts
Things to remember on Election Day 2012

OBAMA says he's the representative for change...He's historic, alright - Check out the changes below:

- First U.S. President to refuse to show a valid Birth Certificate.
- First President to apply for college aid as a foreign student, then deny he was a foreigner
- First President to have a social security number from a state he's never even lived in
- First President to Preside over a Cut to the Credit Rating of the United States Government
- First President to Violate the War Powers Act
- First President to Orchestrate the Sale of Murder Weapons to Mexican Drug Cartels

- First President to be Held in Contempt of Court for Illegally Obstructing Oil Drilling in the Gulf of Mexico
- First President to Defy a Federal Judge's Court Order to Cease Implementing the 'Health Care Reform' Law
- First President to Require All Americans to Purchase a Product from a Third Party
- First President to Spend a Trillion Dollars on 'Shovel-Ready' Jobs-- and Later Admit There Was No Such Thing as Shovel-Ready Jobs
- First President to Abrogate Bankruptcy Law to Turn Over Control of Companies to His Union Supporters
- First President to Bypass Congress and Implement the DREAM Act through Executive Fiat
- First President to "Order a Secret Amnesty Program that Stopped the Deportations of Illegal Immigrants across the US, Including Those with Criminal Convictions"
- First President to Demand a Company Hand Over $20 Billion to One of His Political Appointees
- First President to Terminate America's Ability to Put a Man into Space
- First President to Encourage Racial Discrimination and Intimidation at Polling Places
- First President to Have a Law Signed By an 'Auto-pen' Without Being "Present"
- First President to Arbitrarily Declare an Existing Law Unconstitutional and Refuse to Enforce It
- First President to Threaten Insurance Companies if they publicly speak out on the Reasons for their Rate Increases

- First President to Tell a Major Manufacturing Company in Which State They Are Allowed to Locate a Factory
- First President to File Lawsuits against the States He Swore an Oath to Protect (AZ, WI, OH, IN, etc)
- First President to Withdraw an Existing Coal Permit That Had Been Properly Issued Years Ago
- First President to Fire an Inspector General of Ameri-corps for Catching One of His Friends in a Corruption Case
- First President to Propose an Executive Order Demanding Companies Disclose Their Political Contributions to bid on Government Contracts
- First President to appoint 45 'czars' to replace elected officials in his office.
- First President to Golf 73 separate Times in His First Two-and-a-Half Years in Office
- First President to hide his medical, educational, and travel records
- First President to win a Nobel Peace Prize for doing NOTHING to earn it
- First President to coddle America's enemies while alienating America's allies
- First President to publicly bow to Americas enemies while refusing to salute the US flag
- First President to go on multiple Global apology tours but remember: he will not rest until all Americans have jobs, affordable homes, green-energy vehicles, and the environment is repaired, etc, etc
- First President to go on 17 'vacations', including 'date nights' paid for by the taxpayer.

This speaks volumes also about those who voted for him as they are easily hoodwinked. Scary!

In my opinion Obama's problem is obvious

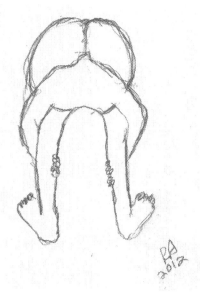

Take heed, if you have not voted or been involved in selecting our countries leaders at the federal, state and local levels, you are BETRAYING America.

If you do not get involved and help correct the situation America as our founding fathers envisioned will be gone in the next generation. Americans will become a minority in a country swamped by illegal foreign criminals. If the Democrats manage to grant amnesty to the illegal criminal aliens like they are trying, America will be lost by the next generation.

CHAPTER 2
ILLEGAL IMMIGRATION

Let us take a look at the problem of illegal immigration. It is one of the most important issues facing Americans today. America is being overrun by foreign human debris and criminals. We have an infestation of undesirables to whom the liberals want to grant amnesty and citizenship.

Strings of garbage across our landscape, and illegals are in shipping containers and are being hidden trucks sneaking into America. ' This needs to stop.

Congress wake up, we are being swamped with undesirables sneaking across our borders.

The Supreme Court must uphold their decision of long ago. 83 US 36 (1873) The "Slaughter-House Cases" "Elk vs. Wlkins" 112 US 94 (1884) the court ruled that people here illegally were not under American jurisdiction. They were subjects of foreign governments. Their offspring born here were subjects of a foreign government not America. The court must enforce those rulings and declare null and void all citizenship granted to "anchor babies" born to illegal immigrants. Then order the immediate deportation of the parents and the child(ren). The Constitution has been erroneously applied far too long.

America has very specific laws and rules for immigrating to America. In my opinion, any person who has not followed these guidelines is a lawbreaker and plainly put is a criminal that should be deported immediately.

Back during the great depression, President Herbert Hoover ordered to immediate deportation of ALL illegal immigrants to make jobs available to the American citizens that desperately needed the work. The illegals were promptly deported. We are in a similar situation now but our president does seem to have the guts to kick these criminals out of America.

After World War II, President Harry Truman deported over two million illegal immigrants to protect jobs of returning war veterans.

In 1954, President Eisenhower, deported 1.3 million illegal immigrants. The program was called "Operation Wetback" it was done so WWII and Korean Veterans could have jobs. The operation took two years, but they deported them.

We need a president that has the courage and fortitude to deport these criminals. Remember to ask the candidates that run in the 2012 election if they have the guts to kick these criminals out of America?

Some of our liberal state governors are actually trying to get laws passed so that illegal's can attend state colleges for the same price as legal citizens.

This Investigative Article from a Los Angeles Paper should open your eyes further.

- 40% of all workers in L.A. County are working for cash and not paying taxes. This is because they are predominantly illegal aliens working without a green card. L.A. County has 10.2 million people.

- 95% of warrants for murder in Los Angeles are for illegal aliens.
- 75% of the people on the most wanted list in Los Angeles are illegal aliens.
- Over 2/3 of all births in Los Angeles County are to illegal alien Mexicans on Medi-Cal, whose births were paid by the taxpayers.
- Nearly 35% of all inmates in California detention centers are Mexican Nationals here illegally.
- Over 300,000 illegal aliens in Los Angeles County are living in garages
- The F.B.I. reports half of all gang members in Los Angeles County are most likely illegal aliens from south of the border
- Nearly 60% of all occupants of HUD Properties are illegal aliens.
- 21 radio stations in Los Angeles are Spanish speaking.
- In Los Angeles County 5.1 million people speak English 3.9 speak Spanish.

Small wonder that California is in the financial mess it's in. Half of its people are paying the whole cost of government.

Less than 2% of illegal aliens are harvesting our crops, but 29% are on welfare. Over 70% of the United States' annual population growth (and over 90% of California, Florida and New York) results from illegal immigration. 29% of inmates in federal prisons are illegal aliens.

My opinion is that the Current U.S. Congress is too cowardly and irresponsible to take on the illegal immigration problem. When a state tries to act on the problem, like Arizona, The federal Government is using my tax money is trying to stop them from solving the problem in their state

Subject: What if 20 million illegal aliens vacated America

(Note: ILLEGAL - here without papers, or in other words criminals)

'They (illegal aliens) pay rent, buy groceries, buy clothes mostly with welfare money...What Happens to your country's economy if 20 million people go away?' Hummm, what would happen, so due diligence was done, into the FACTS found below?

It's a good question - it deserves an honest answer. Over 80% of Americans demand secured borders and illegal migration stopped. But what would happen if all 20 million or more vacated America?

The answers may surprise you!

In California, if 3.5 million illegal aliens left this country, it would leave an extra $10.2 billion to spend on overloaded school systems, bankrupt hospitals and overrun prisons. It would leave highways cleaner, safer and less congested. Everyone could understand one another as English became the dominant language again. And Americans would not have to compete against illegal's' for jobs and employers' would not have a cheap source of labor to pay less than minimum wage.

In Colorado, thousands of illegal migrants, plus their thousands of kids and grand-kids – be deported, mostly to Mexico. That would save Coloradans an estimated $2 billion (other experts say $7 billion) annually in taxes that pay for schooling, medical, social-services and incarceration costs.

It means thousands of gang members would vanish out of Denver alone.

Colorado would save more than $20 million in prison costs, and the terror that those 7,300 alien criminals set upon local citizens.

Denver Public Schools would not suffer a high percent drop-out/flunk-out rate because of thousands of illegal alien students speaking many different languages. Many vehicles would vanish from our gridlocked cities in Colorado. Denver's unemployment rate would vanish as our working poor would gain jobs at a living wage.

In Florida, 1.5 million illegal's, would return the Sunshine State back to America, the rule of law, and English.

In Chicago, Illinois, 2.1 million illegal's being deported would free up hospitals, schools, prisons and highways for a safer, cleaner and more crime-free experience.

If 20 million illegal aliens returned 'home' --

If 20 million illegal aliens returned 'home', the U.S. Economy would return to the rule of law. Employers would hire legal American citizens at a living wage. Everyone would pay their fair share of taxes because they wouldn't be working off the books. That would result in additional hundreds of Billion in IRS income taxes collected annually, and an equal amount for local, state and city coffers.

No more push '1' for Spanish or '2' for English. No more confusion in American schools that now must contend with many foreign languages that degrade the educational system for American kids. Our over-crowded schools would lose more than two million illegal alien kids at a cost of billions in ESL and free breakfasts and lunches.

We would lose 500,000 illegal criminal alien inmates at a cost of more than $1.6 billion annually. That includes the gang members who distribute an estimated $130 billion in drugs annually would be deported out of our country.

In cities like L.A., deporting criminal aliens from our nation would mean; No more Mexican forgery gangs for ID theft from Americans! No more foreign rapists and child molesters! NO more drug dealers, Etc;

Losing more than 20 million people would clear up our crowded highways and gridlock. Cleaner air and less drinking and driving American deaths by illegal aliens!

America's economy is drained. Taxpayers are harmed. Employers get rich. Billions of dollars annually wouldn't be sent out of America to the aliens' home countries by cash transfers.

Illegal migrants earned half that money untaxed, which further drains America's economy - which currently suffers a mutli-trillion dollar debt.

At least 400,000 "anchor babies" would not be born in our country, costing us $109 billion per year per cycle. At least 86 hospitals in California, Georgia and Florida would still be operating instead of being bankrupt and out of existence because illegal's pay nothing via the "EMTALA Act". This act passed by the U.S. Congress forced hospitals to accept people that cannot possibly pay for their care. Other Americans have to pay for them with increased health care insurance costs and medical services while illegal aliens get free medical care.

Americans wouldn't suffer thousands of TB and hepatitis cases rampant in our country-brought in by illegal are unscreened at our borders. The current bedbug epidemic has been traced to illegal immigration. In one major city, five cases of HIV infected women have been traced to one illegal immigrant from African who is HIV positive and also impregnated three of the women.

By enforcing our laws, we could send them back where they came from. We could send 20 million aliens home, to pollute their own countries. We already invite a million people into our country legally more than all other countries combined annually. We cannot and must not allow anarchy at our borders, more anarchy within our borders and growing lawlessness at every level in our nation. It's time to stand up for our country, our culture, our civilization and our way of life.

Interesting Statistics!

Here are some more reasons illegal aliens should be deported from America, and I hope they are read over and over again until they are read so many times that the reader gets sick of reading them:

- Billions of dollars are spent each year on welfare to illegal aliens.

- Billions of dollars are spent each year on food assistance programs such as food stamps, WIC, and free school lunches for illegal aliens. Billions of dollars are spent each year on Medicaid for illegal aliens.
- Billions of dollars are spent each year on primary and secondary school education for children here illegally and they still cannot speak a word of English!
- Billions of dollars are spent each year for education for the American-born children of illegal aliens, known as anchor babies. The U.S. Supreme Court has ruled twice that children born of illegal immigrants are not Automatically American citizens. The 14th Amendment to the U.S. Constitution has been incorrectly applied
- Billions of dollars are spent to incarcerate illegal aliens.
- Billions of dollars are spent each year on illegal aliens for welfare & social services by the American taxpayers.
- Billions dollars per year in suppressed American wages are caused by the illegal aliens.

The illegal aliens in the United States have a crime rate that's far higher than Americans.

During the year 2005, there were 8 to 10 MILLION illegal aliens that crossed our southern border with as many as 19,500 illegal aliens from other terrorist countries. Over 10,000 of those were middle-eastern terrorists.

Millions of pounds of drugs, cocaine, meth, heroine, crack, Guns, and marijuana crossed into the U.S. from the southern border. –

The National Policy Institute estimates that the total cost of mass deportation would be between $206 and $230 billion, or an average cost of between $41 and $46 billion annually over a five year period.

Illegal aliens sent home BILLIONS in remittances back to their countries of origin, to their families & friends.

I believe that deporting the illegal immigrants is going to take a force of arms in many instances. The lawlessness in some of our major cities is rampant among the illegal's'. The armed drug dealers have been making a fortune and they won't go out easily. (Unless we legalize and control drugs)

The liberal "do-gooder liberals" would scream loudly and file lawsuits and jump up and down publicly for the poor criminal aliens.

If these facts don't bother you then continue to ignore the problem and don't vote or help choose our public leaders that are supposed to take care of the illegal immigration problem. But in a few more years, at the rate of illegal immigration, Americans will become the minority in America. Think about that!

Three of our past Presidents had the courage to kick out the illegal's for the benefit of Americans. In my opinion, our current president is too stupid and cowardly to kick out the illegal immigrants. Some of the illegal immigrants are his relatives. His aunt from Kenya here illegally has been living in free government housing long after being ordered deported and his uncle from Kenya (his father's brother) was arrested for drunk driving in Massachusetts and had a driver's license, social security card and he is here illegally. He was ordered to be deported years ago.

What the hell are the immigration people thinking? Why are they not doing their job?

I have no problem with people who wish to immigrate to America and become honest citizens. America was populated with immigrants. We allow more than one million legal immigrants each year, more than all other nations combined. Those people who sneak in illegally and become burdens to the American Taxpayers need to be stopped and those already here, need to be deported immediately.

You as American (hopefully registered voters) should be closely listening to the political candidates and ask them if they will act to kick out the criminals from our America.

CHAPTER 3
FIXING THE PROBLEM

The problem with Government as it is today, it is badly broken and it needs fixing. It is being run by a bunch amoral lobbyists and amoral career politicians. Our State Governors can call for a constitutional convention. And repair our broken government. Pray to God that they have the courage to do so. It only takes 38 state governors to call for a constitutional convention.

We need a Constitutional Convention convened with the following agenda;

- To pass all of these Constitutional Amendments.
- Eliminate the U.S. Senate entirely. It has become, for the most part, an elite, amoral social club full of presidential wanna-bes, and over paid career politicians. It needs to be eliminated and transfer all the rights and responsibilities to the House of Representatives. To be known as The United States Congress. And Then:
- Create two types of representatives. Assign four (4) members to each state geographically as members-at-large (200) the balance would be assigned to contiguously generated districts allocated by

population. One member should go to each of the American Protectorates, American Samoa, and Puerto Rico Etc; with one Assigned to represent Washington D.C. This division would balance geographic interests with population interests.

- Each Member of this unicameral congress would be limited to serve no more than two (2) Four (4) year terms. With all elections for congress being held in the off year from the presidential election.

- Pass a constitutional amendment that denies congress the right to exempt its body from any laws or rules that all the American Citizens must follow.

- Make the Congress immediately use only Social Security for their retirement or purchase their own retirement plan and their medical plan shall be Medicare. *Cancel ALL previous pensions and benefits as they were created only in the greedy self-interest of Congress.*

- Make each member of congress that votes for a deficit budget personally liable for the money in the deficit and not eligible to run for re-election. Except in time of a declared war

- Enact a law, that any member of congress caught lying shall be immediately impeached. It is a Felony Crime for a citizen to lie to congress. Our Congress must to be held to that same standard about lying to the American People.

- Eliminate the Electoral College and honor the vote of the people. Let the people truly choose by the ballot box. More than once in our history of elections, the candidate receiving the most popular votes cast by the American Voters was not the winner after the debacle of the Electoral College.

- Eliminate the income tax and the internal revenue service. Implement a national sales tax and a flat rate tax exempting only some basic essential items like food, clothing, education, medical care or other vital needs. Place a flat rate tax on earnings of more than $200,000.00.

All of the federal Judges must be put up for retention by the voters in their districts at each four year congressional election. No more life time appointments. With the exception of the U.S. Supreme Court.

Congress may not pass any unfunded mandates on any Americans.

Any person in the congress or running for election to the unicameral congress must disclose publicly all support and campaign contributions. Failure to do so would be grounds for immediate dis-qualification from election or immediate impeachment from office.

All members of the congress must report all contacts with lobbyists or anyone else trying to influence them on a weekly basis that is open to for public for review. They must report within 48 hours of receiving any contact or benefits coming to them from lobbyists. Failure to do so will be grounds for impeachment.

If all of these amendments were to be implemented, America would start returning to what our founding Fathers envisioned when they wrote our constitution. A citizen legislature instead of the bunch amoral career politicians we have now. This restructure of our government would solve the gridlock that Americans now suffer through with the two house system.

Take heed, if you have not voted or been involved in selecting our countries leaders at the federal, state and local levels, you are BETRAYING America and your fellow Americans.

CHAPTER #4
HOMOSEXUALITY

Earlier in American history when the Church of Jesus Christ of Latter Day Saints came in to being, they tried Polygamy. The Mormons were reviled and persecuted and society and the courts of law forced upon them the edict that marriage was one man and one woman. The courts upheld that edict repeatedly on all the appeals both state and federal.

Today, Polygamists are reviled and criminally prosecuted whenever they can be found. Again, those prosecuting are using the edict that marriage is between one man and one woman. Several states have passed legislation and state constitutional amendments forbidding the Homosexual, polyandrous and corporate marriages.

Today in our society, we find homosexuals demanding that they are an exception to the rule of marriage as one man and one woman. I find it hard to believe that homosexuality is normal.

Our society in America is founded on Judeo Christian beliefs. I have searched carefully through the Torah and more than one version of the bible, and I found nothing that condones or accepts homosexual marriage.

I can understand allowing some type of civil union so homosexuals can partake in certain benefits that are routinely granted to traditional married couples. But beyond that, I believe that the Judeo/Christian principles that America was founded on do not include anywhere a provision for a "marriage" between homosexuals. From what I have read and seen, homosexuals can and do establish strong emotional bonding between same sex people. I firmly believe that homosexual couples should be allowed to partake of the same fringe benefits of normal married men and women. Provide them some sort of a civil union for the public records.

Homosexuals in the military should receive every right and benefit without prejudice that every other member of the military receives. Those in our armed forces are all volunteers and are our nations' defenders. They live under the blanket of American Freedom and sexual orientation should not be an issue. Members of the armed forces must do their duty without regard to sexual orientation.

In many countries, homosexuality is a capital crime. America is tolerant of many freedoms. Religion, politics, national origin, race, and sexual orientation are all tolerated. The constitution guarantees that "All men are created equal".

CHAPTER #5
THE UNITED STATES
SUPREME COURT

In my opinion, there are number of issues that are facing or should to be facing the U.S. Supreme Court;

Abortion is a no-win situation. I do not condone abortion, but, I worked in the emergency medical service before "Roe v Wade" and I witnessed firsthand the butchery that desperate women suffered. I agree with Justice Ruth Bader Ginzberg, in that a woman's right to privacy of her body is absolute and inviolate. Until the Court makes that ruling, and sets that absolute precedent in legal concrete, the strife over abortion will continue with no winners. Before "Roe v Wade", rich girls got "cultural junkets" to Scandinavia and some girls had "vacation" trips to Mexico and poor women ended up with the back alley butchers. Abortion must be eliminated by persuasion and logic and help for women that suffer unwanted pregnancy.

That Marriage in America is one man and one woman. Several of the states have already passed state constitutional amendments clearly stating this rule.

I believe in freedom of the press absolutely, but some our media in America, have shown that they are more interested in making the news than reporting the news. Some of the media goes to great lengths to write "facts" that are on their face true but omit vital facts that tell the true story. The media, including all print media and all electronic media, shall be held to the highest standard of truth, completeness and fairness. Omitting facts, or information that hold writing in false light by the omission shall be actionable for gross negligence and defamation. America's media must be held to the highest standards of truth and ethical conduct.

The Supreme Court must uphold their decision of long ago. 83 US 36 (1873) The "Slaughter-House Cases" "Elk vs. Wlkins" 112 US 94 (1884) the court must declare null and void all citizenship granted to "anchor babies" born to illegal immigrants and immediately deport the parents and the child(ren). The constitution has been erroneously applied far too long. The liberals will scream at this but it is time to start putting Americans first and stop catering to criminals. Deporting millions of these criminal illegal aliens would go a long way to solving our current unemployment crisis. If our immigration laws are broken, fix them. But stop the illegal horde of criminals invading America.

Chapter #6
The media crisis

First, I believe in the freedom of speech, and freedom of the press. I also believe firmly that with those rights comes the responsibility of the truth, the whole truth, factually, without bias or prejudice.

Political correctness is a doctrine that is fostered by a, delusional, illogical minority, and rabidly promoted, by an unscrupulous mainstream media, that holds forth the proposition, that it is entirely possible to pick a turd by the clean end. I hope this book will help debunk that notion.

I heard a story involving the print media that will illustrate how biased and foul some of our media in America has become.

The story goes

A biker was riding by the zoo, when he saw a little girl leaning into the lion's cage. Suddenly the lion grabs her by her sleeve and tries to pull her into the cage to kill her, all under the eyes of her screaming parents.

The biker jumps off of his bike, jumps into the cage and hits the lion with a powerful punch in the nose. The lion backed up and the biker grabbed the little girl and leaped out of the cage. The little girl's parents thank him tearfully for saving their little girl.

A newspaper reporter has seen the whole event. The reporter addressing the biker says, "Sir that was the most gallant and bravest thing I ever saw a man do in my whole life".

The reporter says, "Well I will make sure that you are recognized for your bravery and quick action". I am a journalist and this will be on the front page. So what do you do for a living and what is you political affiliation?

The Biker replied, I am a "U.S. Marine and a republican".

The next day, the biker bought a morning paper and was shocked by the headline.

"U.S Marine Assaults African Immigrant and steals his Lunch"

Is the American Media that biased and skewed? From personal experience in dealing with the various, I found some of it worse than that. When I was working on the ballot initiative mandate school vouchers, I was attacked personally for items that had no bearing on the voucher issue. I had a permit to carry a concealed handgun. I was attacked by the media as a right wing radical trying to undermine our children's education. The ballot initiative for school vouchers passed by a two to one margin.

It seems remarkable to me that after Tiger Woods crashed his Escalade, the press managed to locate every woman he had an affair with accompanied by photo, text messages, and phone calls. They knew which golf club his wife used to break the window ion his crashed Escalade. Each day they gave Americans updates on his sex addiction rehab and his wife's plans for a divorce. The kept track of the tournaments he was scheduled to play in, dates and places.

Obama has been in office for years and the media still cannot seem to find any of his childhood friends or neighbors. They cannot seem to figure out how he paid for an expensive Harvard Education or any of his college papers or his wife's thesis on racism. They cannot seem to find out what country issued his first passport to travel to Pakistan in the 1980's.

But if you want your personal history and any gaffes you may have made in your life, all you have to do is file for public office as a Republican.

Wake up Americans, you are being screwed by the liberal press members that want to create a socialistic America and pay for it with your tax money. The conduct of the politicians and bureaucrats in Washington D.C. should receive the same attention that Tiger Woods and Sarah Palin received. In depth investigation and a loud hue and cry to the American Public just how bad they are getting screwed.

By writing this book, I am throwing out a challenge to our American Media, both print and electronic, to be professionals and give the American Public the truth, the whole truth and nothing but the truth without prejudice or bias. Dig into some of the issues that I have brought up in this book and tell the Americans just how badly their government is screwing them.

A strong America depends on an honest, truthful and un-biased media. I believe it is the responsibility of the media to report the truth, the whole truth and nothing but the truth.

Post "Watergate", law schools were required to teach ethics in their curriculum. Maybe it is time to include ethics in our journalism classes in America.

To find more about a biased media, read Jesse Ventura's book "Do I stand Alone".

CHAPTER #7
THE FEDERAL JUDICIARY

Appointing Federal judges for a life time has placed them beyond the reach of the citizenry. The federal Judiciary has, in my opinion, corrupted many of our Principles upon which America was founded. The ruling against prayer in school, the ruling against display of Nativity Scenes in public, the ruling against the display of the Ten Commandments on public buildings, the failure to support gun ownership. Just to name a few.

In my opinion, some of the judges appointed were chosen for their political value and personal views rather than their expertise in applying the laws of America and the U.S. Constitution. In reviewing some of the decisions of the San Francisco District Appellate Court, I see many of their decisions being overturned by the U.S. Supreme Court. Yet these judges are beyond the reach of the American voters and I believe that must change.

In my opinion, the first federal judge that ruled against optional prayer in our schools should have been impeached immediately and disbarred from the practice of law for life.

But, in my opinion, our Congress is too cowardly and irresponsible to uphold the U.S Constitution and the laws of America by impeaching these judges.

Until we change our government's structure, the problem with federal judiciary will continue and not in the best interest of the American People.

CHAPTER #8
THE DRUG PROBLEM
IN AMERICA

America did not learn the most valuable lesson from the "Volstead Act" that you cannot successfully legislate away any substance that the people want. The underground drug economy in America is currently running into the hundreds of billions of dollars. This is enough money, to retire our national debt in a few short years. Truck loads of hundred dollar bills leaving this country have been intercepted by law enforcement and this is only a small part of the illegal flow of money out of the country.

The majority of our penal institution occupants are drug-related. The majority our law enforcement and court system expenses are drug related.

What is the solution? We must legalize recreational drugs and closely regulate their use. The American tobacco industry would produce Marijuana cigarettes in a heartbeat. The American Farmers would produce a marijuana and opium poppy crop as easy as they grow corn, soybeans and other food staples. This would take the huge profit out of the illegal drug trade and remove the mystique of illegal drug use. Then drug users could buy needed drugs to support an addiction at the corner drug store, for a token payment. Legalization coupled with a massive and comprehensive anti-drug education program beginning in early childhood, the drug problem in America would be over and gone in less than one generation.

The next step is to make the illegal drug trade a capital offense with vigorous enforcement. The enforcement of the death penalty would be a deterrent in itself and would certainly eliminate repeat offenders.

If this solution sounds harsh, take a good look at the drug wars in Mexico and other countries with the beheadings, public assassinations and murder of law enforcement people and innocent citizens.

If we do not legalize drugs the financial toll on the American Tax payers for the conduct of our current futile drug war will continue to be a drain of vital public resources needed elsewhere.

With legalization, we could divert the funds from law enforcement and the court system into the massive drug education/prevention program against the use of drugs and their effects on the individual and on society. The tax on these drugs, like the alcohol tax, could help balance to budget. Instead this money is going to foreign cartels and some has been traced to funding of some of the foreign terrorist groups. As I am writing this book, the U.S. Coast Guard captured a smuggler's submarine in the Caribbean Sea that contained tons of cocaine worth many millions of dollars on the black market. Wake up Americans, the recreational drugs must be legalized and closely controlled just like alcohol.

Until our U.S. Irresponsible Congress is willing to take the much needed drastic steps, the drug problem in America will continue and the hundreds of billions of dollars will continue to flow out of the country.

Take heed, if you have not voted or been involved in selecting our countries leaders at the federal, state and local levels, you are BETRAYING America and our founding fathers.

Chapter #9
The Two Party Systems

The two major parties in America have taken every step possible to eliminate any competition from a third party or any independent candidates. The result has been career politicians some with more than thirty years in congress.

Our current crisis in government has occurred on this career politicians watch. Deficit spending, outrageous taxes, illegal immigration, bloated duplicate federal government agencies, Etc;

We need to establish a law that the two top vote recipients in the primary election without regard parties shall run in the general election. If any candidate receives a majority (50%+1) of the votes cast in the primary, that candidate shall be declared the winner without running in the general election. In my opinion, the "Electoral College" is an archaic holdover that too often ignores the wishes of the American Voting People.

American voters cannot get together and choose an independent candidate for national office without the being either a Republican or Democrat or one of the minor token "splinter" parties. An American citizen that wants to run for president as an independent is in for an uphill battle just to get on the ballot. The liberal media would tear an independent candidate to shreds to protect heir "Poster Boy".

One of the solutions that might be considered is that all campaign contributions for a given office must be pooled and distributed equally among the candidates. That includes both the primary and general elections.

Two of most noteworthy independent public office holders were Governor Angus King of Maine and Governor Jesse Ventura of Minnesota. These two are the only independents elected to a major public office at the state level. Both were attacked repeatedly by the media and the two major parties. Even though both tried several reforms that would have saved the taxpayers millions of dollars, they could get no support for their efforts from either of the two parties. The two major parties considered them both as outcasts that were a threat to their democrat or republican parties.

Jesse Ventura proposed a unicameral legislature for Minnesota and the politicians and the media attacked him viciously for his effort to save the taxpayers Hundreds of thousands of dollars annually and streamline the state government. . He was attacked viciously by both parties. The thought of career politicians losing office was terrifying.

The State of Kansas has had a unicameral legislature for many years and it operates very efficiently. In other states where unicameral legislatures have been considered, the incumbent politicians have resisted it with every means possible. The thought of losing office by career politicians' is terrifying. Look at the money it would save the taxpayers! Look at how many career politicians it would eliminate.

The unicameral system of a legislative body eliminates the common finger pointing back and forth that Americans have to tolerate now. It would also eliminate the U.S. Senate and the hundreds of billions of dollars of drain on the American taxpayer.

Some practical form of nomination for national office must be established for the citizens to use and not be controlled by either of the Republicans or Democrats. The tragedy of choosing candidates for national office is that most of the well qualified people do not want any part of being elected due to the cess pool of amoral politics in Washington D.C.

One prime example from the past is Lee Iacocca. He turned Chrysler Corporation Around and paid back the government loan early. When he was approached to run for president he emphatically declined.

I was talking to a well known lawyer some years ago and I asked him why he didn't run for the state senate. He carefully explained to me that he owned several of them why should he want to be one.

James Madison, in the "Federalist Paper #10" cautioned against the Peril of two party systems. He warned of the strife between two factions becoming the purpose of their existence and the needs of the Americans taking second place to the parties first interest of being the dominate party. With the two party system. Currently in our nation's capital, the American people are in second place behind party politic loyalty. It is time for America to switch to a unicameral legislature, get rid of career politicians and streamline our American Government.

As I am writing this, protestors are marching on Wall Street and several other locations. My advice is to wake up and choose some of your group as candidates and collect the signatures on a petition that our current government requires for a citizen to run for public office. Get some people on the inside of our Washington Cabal and start to take back America from the inside. The U.S. Congress has to run for re-election every two years. If you start now in four years, you, the concerned public, could take back control of you government and your future destiny.

I believe that more than 50% of registered American voters are registered as non-aligned. Independent, undeclared, nonpartisan etc; I believe they are ripe for a viable independent presidential candidate to step forward and lead our nation. Maybe Jesse Ventura would step forward?

If an independent Presidential candidate was to arise from the middle of America, I believe that the chance for election to the presidency in 2012 would be very high. I believe that for the first time in history, a "write-in" candidate could win the American Presidency.

America this may be your chance to form the "Responsible Party" and start taking back America.

As Lee Iacocca writes in his book "Where Have All the Leaders Gone" he is wondering where are the leaders of our American society that could step forward in front of the American people and lead our nation back to the path our forefathers envisioned.

Take heed, if you have not voted or been involved in selecting our countries leaders at the federal, state and local levels, you are BETRAYING America.

Chapter #10
Liberals vs. Conservative

- If a conservative doesn't like guns, he doesn't buy one.
- If a liberal doesn't like guns, he wants all guns outlawed.
- If conservative is a vegetarian, he doesn't eat meat.
- If a liberal is a vegetarian, he wants all meat products banned for everyone.
- If a conservative is a homosexual, he quietly leads his life.
- If a liberal is a homosexual, he demands legislated respect.
- If a conservative is down and out, he figures out how to better himself on his own.
- If a liberal is down and out, he demands to know who is going to take care of him.
- If a conservative doesn't like a talk show host, he changes channel and doesn't watch the show.
- Liberals demand that those they don't like or agree with be shut down.
- If a conservative is a non-believer, he doesn't go to church.

- If a liberal is a non-believer, he wants all mention of religion silenced.
- If a conservative needs health care, he goes shopping for it or takes a job where it is included.
- A liberal demands that the rest of us pay for his.
- If a conservative slips and falls in a store, he gets up embarrassed and laughs about it.
- If a liberal slips and falls in a store, he grabs his neck and groans and then sues.
- If a conservative reads this comparison, he will laugh about it and show it to his friends.
- If a liberal reads this comparison, he will be offended. Good!

The liberals are responsible for giving away our Social Security Trust fund to illegal immigrants. This action stole the money in trust for American contributors to retire on and gave it to illegal immigrants and immigrants that had not contributed anything to the Trust. In my opinion, this was a blatant violation of trust and a theft from American People that counted on their trust fund for retirement.

We need to eliminate the Liberal vs. Conservative Dogma. We should instead refer to our politicians as "responsible". If our politicians were responsible, we would not be in the mess America is in currently. If a political wannabe proves to be not responsible, eliminate him or her from public office. Our political leaders must learn to put Americans first. The American cannot continue to take second place in our congressional agenda.

CHAPTER #11
LOBBYING CONGRESS,
THE PAYOFF

Three of the major special interests lobbing the U.S Congress in 2009, spent $3.49 Billion dollars that they admit to.

With 535 members of Congress, that equals about:

$3,490,000,000 divided by 535 = $6,535,000.00 for each and every member of congress. America has the best congress that money can buy!

The Pharmaceutical Industry, Healthcare industry, and the Doctor's Lobby are also some of the other leading spenders followed by labor unions. The Agriculture Industry, Auto Industry, Communication Industry, Education Lobby, Lumber Industry, Mining Industry, Shipping Industry, Energy Industry, Finance Industry etc; Each of these industries spend millions more to influence the congress. Not to mention the "fact finding junkets" taken in corporate jets to places that just happen to be premiere vacation spots with luxurious golf courses and perfect climates. I wonder if a "fact finding trip" to the Caribbean Islands in the winter time just might be too convenient.

Have you ever wondered how incumbent congressional people can raise tens of millions dollars for re-election to a job that pays less than $200,000 annually? Who do you think your representative is going to listen to, you, the constituent, or the people who walk in the door with a multimillion dollar "campaign contributions"? The answer is simple in my opinion; they have sold their souls to get re-elected. Their constituents are getting the shaft.

With the money spent lobbying by the Financial Industry, the Insurance and the Real Estate industry, do you wonder why the thieves that stole to share holders blind with exorbitant bonuses, lavish salaries and extravagant parties have not been thoroughly investigated and punished.

The answer is simple, in my Opinion, they own the U.S. Congress. Special interests own your government. God help the American Taxpayer, you haven't got a chance.

Maybe we need to pass a law that all lobbying money is put into a trust fund and distributed equally among all the candidates at the next election.

Earlier in this book, I proposed that America should go to a unicameral congress with strict term limits. I hope that as you read through the conduct of our politicians, that you will see the wisdom and support streamlining our government. The state governors can call for a constitutional convention and I believe that the American People would support taking back their country. What a change in government that would bring.

It may sound like a radical change, but a unicameral legislature would save the American Taxpayer Billions of dollars every year. The gridlock caused by the two politically posturing bodies would be eliminated. When a unicameral member reached the second term with no chance of re-election, I believe that honesty and the best interests of the American People might prevail. A member of congress that has nothing to gain in a re-election should be tough to bribe with campaign contributions. This would be the special interests lobbyists' worst nightmare, Congressional members that had the best interests of American at heart and could not be bribed or bought.

Wow, what a novel idea! A congress that actually had the best interests of the citizens at heart. The billions of dollars being pissed away by the U.S. Senate would stop. With the transparency of term limited politicians, maybe the American Taxpayers would get to be first in line for a change.

Chapter #12
Our Education Dilemma

Since I started to the First Grade in 1948, I have seen a revolutionary change in our schools systems in America.

When I went to school, we saluted the flag every morning and I was proud to do it. My stay in public schools was brief; I ended up with the Jesuits and the Dominicans and then finished with Military Academy. I spent my last two years in public high school basically killing time waiting for college. During these two years, I learned basic carpentry, welding, machine work, electricity and automotive mechanics. My classmates were not so fortunate. Their education was deficient to say the least. I took the college aptitude test and scored in the 98.9% percentile, my closest classmate scored in the 88% percentile. So much for union teaching.

Today, the liberals are trying to eliminate ALL mention of God in our schools, from the flag salute to saying grace at lunch. They seem to forget that America was founded as a Judeo/Christian Nation with belief in God and freedom of religion for all. The shame of this effort to eliminate God from our schools and public places is that the Federal Judiciary has supported it.

When a Federal Judge, in my opinion, denies placement of the Ten Commandments in public schools and buildings and the mention of God in our schools, raises the question about our cowardly and irresponsible U.S. Congress. The U.S. Congress has the power to impeach a Federal Judge for cause. What better cause than undermining our America Judeo/Christian Values?

In my opinion, the teachers unions have done far more harm than they ever did well. I saw incompetent teachers with tenure defended by the unions. I have watched the American Education system decay from the misguided efforts of unions when the unions should have been striving to put forth the best efforts for our children.

I was involved once in a public debate forum on school vouchers. My group was running a ballot initiative to initiate school vouchers. I was defending/proposing them with two other folks and on the other side in the forum; there were three union public school teachers.

When one of my turns to speak came, I told the opposing panel and the audience that, "the teachers should stop fighting the parental right to choose for their children's education. What the teachers union should do is support school vouchers and then make their schools work so well and be so successful that all the parents would line up with their vouchers to send their children to them". It took the moderator several minutes to restore order, the crowd was on their feet shouting and applauding.

When my next turn came to speak, the moderator recognized me. I told the opposing panel, "You cannot legislate yourselves the exclusive right to teach our children and then provide them with a sub-standard education as prescribed by your union dogma". "Our children are America's most valuable resource, they are our future, and they deserve better than you have been giving them or we would not be having this forum tonight. And I would not

Have been able to collect the signatures of 81% of the registered voters in this jurisdiction on a petition to bring in school vouchers". Again, the crowd with standing applause that took several minutes for the moderator to restore order.

When my last turn to speak came, I told the union teachers that if they could not properly educate our children, they should get the hell out of the public facilities and let in the teachers who cared more about our children than they did the teacher's union. Again it took the moderator several minutes to restore order to the room.

What is the answer? In my opinion, students should be tested periodically by a professionally designed comprehensive test to honestly evaluate the individual student. The results of that testing should be most revealing in several ways. First it would help identify the student's needs, aptitudes, achievements, and abilities. Second it would give some indication of the teacher's performance and achievements. By looking at test scores from students from a broad sample group, from a particular teacher, a pattern of performance would become statistically evident.

The next part of our education dilemma is college costs. First, I believe that ALL education costs for college, graduate school, trade school, occupational training, should be 100% tax deductible including the money put aside in education funds. The cost of higher education has risen to levels that are crippling to most students who complete their education facing hundreds of thousands of dollars in student loans.

I see that many college presidents are now demanding multimillion dollar salaries. The president of Harvard University draws a salary of less than one million dollars and gets a house to live in on campus rent free. To the college presidents that have connived to get multimillion dollar salaries, I say shame on you and the people that agreed to pay it. The fact that some college sports coach's are getting multimillion dollar salaries, to me is bordering on criminal greed. What in hell are the school trustees thinking about?

America is the Greatest Nation in the world. If we don't act to restore our education system to what it must be, we will no longer be the example for the rest of the world to follow. We will be reduced to a mediocre education system in a mediocre country. I do not believe that is what Americans want.

I saw this floating around on the internet.

Things have changed drastically since I was in school in the 50's.

HIGH SCHOOL -- 1957 vs. 2010

Scenario 1:

Jack goes quail hunting before school and then pulls into the school parking lot with his shotgun in his truck's gun rack.

1957 - Vice Principal comes over, looks at Jack's shotgun, goes to his car and gets his shotgun to show Jack.

2010 - School goes into lock down, FBI called, Jack hauled off to jail and never sees his truck or gun again. Counselors called in for traumatized students and teachers.

Scenario 2:

Johnny and Mark get into a fist fight after school.

1957 - Crowd gathers. Mark wins. Johnny and Mark shake hands and end up buddies.

2010 - Police called and SWAT team arrives -- they arrest both Johnny and Mark. They are both charged them with assault and both expelled even though Johnny started it.

Scenario 3:

Jeffrey will not be still in his class, he disrupts other students.

1957 - Jeffrey sent to the Principal's office and given a good paddling by the Principal. He then returns to class, sits still and does not disrupt class again.

2010 - Jeffrey is given huge doses of Ritalin. He becomes a zombie. He is then tested for ADD. The family gets extra money (SSI) from the government because Jeffrey has a disability.

Scenario 4:

Billy breaks a window in his neighbor's car and his Dad gives him a whipping with his belt.

1957 - Billy is more careful next time, grows up normal, goes to college and becomes a successful businessman.

2010 - Billy's dad is arrested for child abuse. Billy is removed to foster care and joins a gang. The state psychologist is told by Billy's sister that she remembers being abused her and their dad goes to prison. Billy's mom has an affair with the psychologist.

Scenario 5:

Mark gets a headache and takes some aspirin to school..

1957 - Mark shares his aspirin with the Principal out on the smoking dock

2010 - The police are called and Mark is expelled from school for drug violations. His car is then searched for drugs and weapons.

Scenario 6:

Pedro fails high school English.

1957 - Pedro goes to summer school, passes English and goes to college.

2010 - Pedro's cause is taken up by liberals. Newspaper articles appear nationally explaining that teaching English as a requirement for graduation is racist. ACLU files class action lawsuit against the state school system and Pedro's English teacher. English is then banned from core curriculum. Pedro is given his diploma anyway but ends up mowing lawns for a living because he cannot speak English.

Scenario 7:

Johnny takes apart leftover firecrackers from the Fourth of July, puts them in a model airplane paint bottle and blows up a red ant bed.

1957 - Ants die.

2010 - ATF, Homeland Security and the FBI are all called. Johnny is charged with domestic terrorism. The FBI investigates his parents -- and all siblings are removed from their home and all computers are confiscated. Johnny's dad is placed on a terror watch list and is never allowed to fly again.

Scenario 8:

Johnny falls while running during recess and scrapes his knee He is found crying by his teacher, Mary. Mary hugs him to comfort him.

1957 - In a short time, Johnny feels better and goes on playing.

2010 - Mary is accused of being a sexual predator and loses her job. She faces 3 years in State Prison. Johnny undergoes 5 years of therapy.

America has a shortage of skilled craftsmen thanks to union teaching. Plumbers, electricians, tile setters, automotive technicians (mechanics), cabinet makers, chefs, shoemakers, bakers, roofers, the list is endless. We need to rethink our education system and test our young people and establish what they want to do for a lifelong work career. The teachers' unions have tried to tell every child that they don't have to demean themselves with manual labor, they can all be doctors and lawyers.

For many years, continuing to this day, craft unions have provided apprenticeships for these skills. The unions have declined severely in recent years for a variety of reasons but the demand for skilled craftspeople has increased every year.

If this pisses you off it is time for you to take an active part in solving America's problem. The problem is not going to fix itself and if you don't get involved, someone else is going to keep making decisions like to one described here for you. What do you want for America?

Take heed, if you have not voted or been involved in selecting our countries leaders at the federal, state and local levels, you are BETRAYING America.

CHAPTER #13
TAXES

Americans are being taxed beyond any decent limit and the politicians can't seem to stop spending. They have an addiction to spending the American people's hard earned money. Our politicians have nearly bankrupted America.

Let us look at some of the taxes Americans pay:

- Federal Income tax
- Federal sales tax
- State income tax
- State Sales tax
- City Sales tax
- Property tax
- Communication tax both state and federal
- Alcohol tax state and federal
- Tobacco tax state and federal
- Gasoline tax state and federal
- Corporate tax state and federal
- Dog license tax
- Fuel permit tax
- Social Security tax
- Marriage license tax

- Hunting license tax
- Fishing license
- Inventory tax
- Firearms tax
- Meal tax

This is just a partial list of taxes that Americans have to pay. There are literally hundreds of other state and local taxes not listed here. Some of the taxes have been in existence since the Spanish-American War. Once a tax is placed, getting rid of it is UN- heard of.

The internal revenue service is completely beyond any decent control. They can make a criminal out of you and you have to prove your innocence. They can steal your bank account, garnish your wages, take your vehicle and sell your house, all of this without any due process or court orders.

You can be bankrupted and put out of business by the internal revenue service before you ever get a day in court. The U.S. Congress has allowed this to go on for years to ensure that they have money to spend with little regard how it is collected. The internal revenue service is allowed to operate that way because congress wants it that way. Vicious and illegal while exhorting money for the congress to spend. If the I.R.S. was to be reined in from its criminal conduct, the U.S. Congress would not have to obscene amount of tax payer dollars to piss away. The I.R.S. is going to stay just like it is, vicious and mean because that is the way congress wants it and to hell with the American Taxpayers.

When congress wants more money to spend, they just start eliminating tax deductions. Take for instance the deduction for interest on car loans, credit cards etc; the deduction was eliminated and raised hundreds of billions of dollars and allowed the IRS to tax that money more than once. This is an insidious way to raise taxes seemingly without seeming to raising them. One of the deductions considered for elimination was the home owner's mortgage interest deduction. How many Americans could afford to keep their homes if that deduction was taken away?

One of the other insidious ways governments collect money from citizens is "parking authorities" that are thinly disguised as law enforcement. The main purpose of these is to raise money, not enforce the law. In fact they make the laws so confusing that the public can not comply assuring a plentiful supply of fine money and the piously tell the complainers, "stop breaking the law". The main purpose of law enforcement is to get the public to comply with the law. The last thing these predators want is compliance.

The fairest way to collect taxes, in my opinion, might be to levy a federal sales tax on most items. Food, health care, education, home sales, is of some of the things that might be exempted. Levying a federal sales tax a flat tax would make everybody pay. Such a tax would collect from the underground economy which runs into hundreds of Billions of dollars annually. Placing a sales tax on money orders and credit transfers would collect from those who send money out of the country. The enforcement of a federal sales tax would cost far less than is currently spent on the Internal Revenue Service. By levying a federal sales tax, I believe that 10% might be too high since it would catch so many non-payers. With a sales tax in place, the people who wanted to save their earnings for whatever purpose, retirement, education, to buy a home, etc; could do it without having the federal government taking out taxes before they are due.

The people that earn more than $250,000.00 annually should be taxed at 25% flat rate or some similar number.

I believe that this method of taxation would be an easy sell to a unicameral legislature.

As I am writing this politically un-correct book, the 2012 republican campaign for president has started. I hope that the candidates read this book and particularly this chapter. I believe that I agree on a tax method.. Some of the people do not understand yet that this is a new type of tax to replace the income tax and eliminate the I.R.S...

Think about it American voters. A tax that catches everyone, all the illegal drug dealers have to buy items to live and the underground economy that exists would have to pay their taxes for a change. And you have a chance to save your hard earned money before the government steals part of it. What a concept to consider, fair taxation for everyone. You can save your hard earned money before the government takes any it.

With a national sales tax, and some life sustaining items exempted, such as food, healthcare, and homes, everyone that buys anything has to pay. The people that want to save their money can and not be taxed until they spend it on taxable items. If Herman Cain should read this book, I would hope he will consider what is put forth here.

Chapter #14
Social Security

Let's take a look at the history of Social Security. It was introduced by President Franklin Delano Roosevelt, a Democrat, and he promised:

- That participation in the program would be completely voluntary.
- That the participants would only have to pay 1% of their annual income into the program.
- That the money participants elected to put into the program would be tax deductible from their income tax each year.
- That the money the participants put into the "independent trust fund" rather than into the General operating fund would only be used to fund the Social Security Retirement Program, and no other government Program.
- The promise that the annuity payments would never be taxed as income.

The Rest of the Storey

Since many of us have paid into FICA for years and are now receiving a Social Security Check every month and then finding that we are taxed on 85% of the money we paid into the promised trust fund.

Q. Which Political Party took Social Security from the "Trust Fund" and put it into the government's general fund so that Congress could spend it?

A. It was Lyndon Johnson and the Democratically Controlled House and Senate.

Q. Which Political Party eliminated the income tax deduction for Social Security (FICA) Withholding?

A. The Democratic Party

Q Which Political Party started taxing our Social Security Benefits?

A. the Democratic Party, with Al Gore casting the "Tie breaking" vote as President of the Senate, while he was Vice-President of the U.S. It was not enough that they stole our social security but then the politicians started stealing more by taxing our benefits after we were promised they would never be taxed.

Q. Which Political Party decided to start giving Social Security Benefits to immigrants?

A. That's right! Jimmy Carter and the Democratic Party of course.

Immigrants moved to America and at age 65 began to receive Social Security Benefits. The Democratic Party gave them these payments even though they never paid anything into the American's Trust Fund.

Now after doing all this lying and thieving and violating the original trust promised, the Democrats tell you that the Republicans want to take away your Social Security.

The hundreds of billions of dollars that were in the Social Security Trust fund proved to be too much of a temptation to the politicians. The trust fund that was put aside to guarantee the comfortable retirement of its contributors was, in my opinion, stolen by the politicians. The politicians then started giving the trust fund money to illegal immigrants that had contributed nothing to the fund. I have researched carefully and I can find no indication that any public legal advocate took any action in the judiciary to stop the government from stealing the social security trust fund. I wondered where the hell the ACLU was when all this was going on.

The fact of the matter is that the Democrats stole the social security trust fund and moved it into the general fund so they could spend it. The rest of the story is that when the Republicans regained the majority, instead of restoring the promised trust to the Americans who owned it, they also started spending it. Between the two, they managed to bankrupt the trust fund. So much for integrity in the U.S. Congress.

What needs to happen now is for the congress to be ordered by the U.S. Supreme Court, to restore the trust fund that they stole from the Americans that built the trust fund with their deposits. Replace the trust totally with interest and then keep their damn hands off of it. The trust fund needs to be put under an independent commission free from congressional interference or access and this body would always be subject to audit and full public disclosure.

If our social security fund had been managed like an "ERISA Trust Fund" as the government mandates private industry, instead of being stolen, today it would be solvent and our seniors and other contributors would have complete financial security for their retirement.

What is ERISA?

The Employee Retirement Income Security Act of 1974, or ERISA, protects the assets of millions of Americans so that funds placed in retirement plans during their working lives will be there when they retire.

ERISA is a federal law that sets minimum standards for pension plans in private industry. For example, if an employer maintains a pension plan, ERISA specifies when an employee must be allowed to become a participant, how long they have to work before they have a non-forfeitable interest in their pension, how long a participant can be away from their job before it might affect their benefit, and whether their spouse has a right to part of their pension in the event of their death. Most of the provisions of ERISA are effective for plan years beginning on or after January 1, 1975.

ERISA does not require any employer to establish a pension plan. It only requires that those who establish plans must meet certain minimum standards. The law generally does not specify how much money a participant must be paid as a benefit.

ERISA does the following:

It requires plans to provide participants with information about the plan including important information about plan features and funding. The plan must furnish some information regularly and automatically. Some is available free of charge, some is not.

It sets minimum standards for participation, vesting, benefit accrual and funding. The law defines how long a person may be required to work before becoming eligible to participate in a plan, to accumulate benefits, and to have a non-forfeitable right to those benefits. The law also establishes detailed funding rules that require plan sponsors to provide adequate funding for your plan.

It requires accountability of plan fiduciaries. ERISA generally defines a fiduciary as anyone who exercises discretionary authority or control over a plan's management or assets, including anyone who provides investment advice to the plan. Fiduciaries that do not follow the principles of conduct may be held responsible for restoring losses to the plan.

It gives participants the right to sue for benefits and breaches of a fiduciary duty.

It guarantees payment of certain benefits if a defined plan is terminated, through a federally chartered corporation, known as the Pension Benefit Guaranty Corporation.

If the hundreds of billions of dollars paid into the social security trust fund by American workers had been managed according to "ERISA" Law, today the fund would be a self sustaining fund worth nearly a trillion dollars. The American people who paid into the trust fund could be retired in comfort with a tax free monthly pension as they were originally promised.

There are about 54,605,000 receiving social security benefits (including illegal's and people who contributed nothing to the trust fund) in 2011. If Social Security had been managed like an "ERISA" Trust, today it would be worth more than a trillion dollars. The Monthly payout from a sustained fund would be approximately $2106 monthly. If the illegal immigrants were to be kicked off and deported as they should be, that amount would rise to about an average payout per recipient of an average of $2500 monthly which should be tax free.

Some of the 2012 presidential "wannabes" have claimed that social security is a "Ponzi Scheme". In my opinion, the reason it is where it is right now is because of thieving politicians from both major parties. If all the social security trust funds had been managed like the private retirement funds as required by The Federal "ERISA Act", the owner/contributors to the trust fund would enjoy a worry free retirement instead of a poverty level fixed income shared with illegal aliens that have contributed nothing.

This is take on career politician that was floating around on the internet

Senator Alan Simpson Calls Seniors 'Greediest Generation'.

Hey Alan,

Let's get a few things straight...

1. As a career politician, you have been on the public dole for FIFTY YEARS...

2. I have been paying Social Security taxes for 48 YEARS (since I was 15 years old. I am now 63)...

3. My Social Security payments, and those of millions of other Americans, were safely tucked away in an interest bearing account for decades until you political pukes decided to raid the account and give OUR money to a bunch of zero ambition losers in return for votes, thus bankrupting the system and turning Social Security into a Ponzi scheme that would have made Bernie Madoff proud...

4. Recently, just like Lucy & Charlie Brown, you and your ilk pulled the proverbial football away from millions of American seniors nearing retirement and moved the goalposts for full retirement from age 65 to age 67. NOW, you and your shill commission are proposing to move the goalposts YET AGAIN...

5. I, and millions of other Americans, have been paying into Medicare from Day One, and now you morons propose to change the rules of the game. Why? Because you idiots mismanaged other parts of the economy to such an extent that you need to steal money from Medicare to pay the bills...

I, and millions of other Americans, have been paying income taxes our entire lives, and now you propose

To increase our taxes yet again. Why? Because you incompetent bastards spent our money so profligately that you just kept on spending even after you ran out of money. Now, you come to the American taxpayers and say you need more to pay off YOUR debt…

To add insult to injury, you label us "greedy" for calling "bullshit" on your incompetence. Well, Captain Bullshit, I have a few questions for YOU…

1. How much money have you earned from the American taxpayers during your pathetic 50-year political career?
2. At what age did you retire from your pathetic political career, and how much are you receiving in annual retirement benefits from the American taxpayers?
3. How much do you pay for YOUR government provided health insurance?
4. What cuts in YOUR retirement and health care benefits are you proposing in your disgusting deficit reduction proposal, or, as usual, have you exempted yourself and your political cronies?
5.

It is you, Captain Bullshit, and your political co-conspirators who are "greedy". It is you and they who have bankrupted America and stolen the American dream from millions of loyal, patriotic taxpayers. And for what? Votes. That's right, sir. You and yours have bankrupted America for the sole purpose of advancing your pathetic political careers. You know it, we know it, and you know that we know it.

From the internet:
Social Security entitlement ??????

This is very appropriate in light of what is going on !!! Remember, not only did you contribute to Social Security but your employer did too. It totaled 15% of your income before taxes. If you averaged only 30K over your 49 year working life, that's close to $220,500. If you calculate the future value of $4,500 per year (yours & your employer's contribution) at a simple 5% (less than what the govt. pays on the money that it borrows), after 49 years of working (me) you'd have $892,919.98. If you took out only 3% per year, you would receive $26,787.60 per year and it would last better than 30 years, and that's with no interest paid on that final amount on deposit! If you bought an annuity and it paid 4% per year, you'd have a lifetime income of $2,976.40 per month. The folks in Washington have pulled off a bigger Ponzi scheme than Bernie Madhoff ever had.

Entitlement, my foot, I paid cash for my social security insurance!!!! Just because they borrowed the money, doesn't make my benefits some kind of charity or handout !! Congressional benefits, aka free healthcare, outrageous retirement packages, 67 paid holidays, three weeks paid vacation, unlimited paid sick days, now that's welfare, and they have the nerve to call my retirement entitlements !!!!!! They call Social Security and Medicare an entitlement even though most of us have been paying for it all our working lives and now when it's time for us to collect, the government is running out of money. Why did the government steal it in the first place?

Robert Alan

Take heed, if you have not voted or been involved in selecting our countyy' leaders at the federal, state and local levels, you are BETRAYING America

CHAPTER #15
OUR MILITARY AND
OUR VETERANS

I believe that America has the finest military forces in the world. Our military is made up of people who believe in America. Americans need to say "Thank You" more often and our congress needs to start keeping their promises to them.

Unfortunately, our military is interfered with by too many politicians for them to do their job. Our forces have had to fight wars that they are not allowed to win. If water boarding or other persuasions used by American forces will save one American life, go for it. When I see public beheadings on TV by terrorists and read about suicide bombings killing hundreds of innocent men women and children I personally have no qualms about any method of persuasion on the terrorists'. They do not respect human life or have any decency, so why shouldn't we treat them by the same rules they have chosen?

In my opinion, we had no business invading Iraq. After we did, we should have deposed Saddam Hussein and turned the country over to the Iraqi's and left. There probably would have been a civil war and Iraq would have settled its own destiny.

In my opinion, after our armed forces kicked the Taliban out of Afghanistan, we should have turned the country over to the Afghan People and left. To have stayed and fought the way we have is in my opinion, a no-win situation. We have wasted hundreds of billions of dollars supporting a corrupt government in a country where graft and corruption has been a way of life for centuries. There is no way we can establish a democracy in a Muslim Nation, the religion does not allow it.

Our leaders have tried to establish a democracy in countries where the Islamic Religion forbids it. Enough on that.

Our military is all voluntary and for the job they do and their role in America's Security, they are underpaid. When I hear our Washington Politicians talk about how much our armed forces cost, it makes me ashamed. They are getting a bargain. A lot of our members of the armed forces qualify for food stamps. Our armed forces should be held in the high esteem that they righteously deserve.

Our veterans have had many promises made for health care, education and compensation for injuries received in service to their country. I have been in a VA hospital and they are sadly underfunded and most of them are not equipped to give our veterans the help they need.

The spinoff from these wars has been costly to our military. Our veterans have had the promise of care for them broken many times and in many ways. When I hear about homeless veterans living in the street or in their car, it makes me want ask our U.S. Congress "What the hell are you thinking"? Where is the help and benefits that were promised for these veterans that went in harm's way for America? These are the people that wrote a blank check to America payable up to and including their lives.

From their service comes our American Freedom.

Take heed, if you have not voted or been involved in selecting our countries leaders at the federal, state and local levels, you are BETRAYING America.

CHAPTER #16
OUR WELFARE SYSTEM
IN AMERICA

The government should provide for the national defense, postal service, public education, <u>a self extinguishing welfare system</u> and a law enforcement/ court system.

The law enforcement and court system should include the penal system.

California in the 1960's had third generation welfare recipients that had never had a deposit made to their social security account. They had been born into welfare lived their whole life on welfare and died. The American taxpayers had supported them their whole life.

I remember growing up in rural America and the values I was raised by. You had to work for everything you got nothing was free. Then I remember when liberal social workers were visiting low income people and soliciting them to go on the welfare rolls. Not to supplement their living but to introduce them to a free ride at the working American taxpayers' expense.

Anybody can have a run of misfortune and need a hand up. Welfare must become a helping hand for a time in need and not a way of life. Every welfare recipient in America should have to pass a drug test every week, including nicotine, alcohol, and all illegal drugs before they get their welfare check. If they fail the test or refuse it, they do not get a check. If the recipient wants to use drugs legal or illegal then they can get a job. There needs to be a mandatory work programs and training to bridge the gap between school and a job.

I was in Texas some years ago in a courtroom waiting and I heard a Judge tell a man that he would either show up for work at the city yard or the judge would send him to jail for not supporting his family and he could work on the county chain gang. The sheriff's deputy I was with told me later that the guy left for California with his wife and seven kids because he could just collect welfare and not have to work out there.

Every week that welfare recipients get a check, they should have to go through drug screening and present proof of searching for work or be attending a work training program. The liberals are currently fighting legal battles where drug screening has been made a requirement for welfare. I and thousands of other Americans have gone through pre-employment drug screening. Why shouldn't our welfare recipients have to meet the same standard?

Every time someone applies for welfare, they should get the help they need. Give them a hand in their time of need and put them on the payroll somewhere. If they are sick, heal them, if they are ignorant educate and train them. Cleaning up a public park, tending to public buildings, working with the elderly, Etc; but don't give them a free ride. Every able bodied person in America, men and women, should have to work. If they need training, then train them. If they still won't work, incarcerate them and let them work on a chain gang.

Our welfare case workers must become educators. Many of the people needing welfare are deficient in their education. Deficient from bad personal decisions, early pregnancy, drug problems, family problems, and a sad lack of education into the ways of America. In my opinion, the teachers' unions have been the largest contributor to our welfare population. The people on welfare, some of them are in crisis and need our help. Our welfare case workers need to rise to that challenge and give these folks the guidance to enter the American work force mainstream and become proud citizens.

America's welfare system must not remain a career as it has become in the past. American taxpayers are being ripped off by the liberals in the welfare system. Our U.S. Congress, in my opinion, is too spineless and cowardly to take action to clean up the welfare system. I think a unicameral congress might be more conducive to cleaning up the welfare mess.

If you, the middle class taxpaying citizens, do not register and vote, our crisis in America will only get worse. We need the people that pay for America with their taxes to get involved now.

CHAPTER #17
AMERICAS INFRASTRUCTURE

America in the 1950's, under President Eisenhower, was a country to behold for the rest of the world. Our national highway system was almost completed and the envy of the rest of the world. Since then, we failed to keep up our roads, bridges, dams, public buildings and all other manner of our infrastructure.

Our government has sent trillions of dollars to foreign places in the name of "Foreign Aid" and "Military Aid" while they have let America sink into morass of delayed maintenance, neglect and apathy. The lack of maintenance on our federal highway system is, in my opinion, criminal. There has been a federal fuel tax collected for years that were imposed to maintain our federal highway system. We have dams that are currently unstable and a danger to Americans. Maybe it is time to put America and Americans first. This probably won't happen with our government in its current form.

Our forests have been decimated to less than 10% of what they were when the pilgrims first landed. Our streams and rivers are clogged with debris and by erosion. Our lands have been denuded by strip mining. Our wildlife habitat has been destroyed. Only by the private efforts of America's Sportsmen were our waterfowl brought back from extinction.

Our forests and wild lands should be cared for our descendents, and our children's children. That might be a good place to put a bunch of inmates to work?

I firmly believe that every citizen owes America at least one year of public service excluding the military or in lieu of military service. Similar to the "Civilian Conservation Corps" that was so successful during the great depression.

We have hundreds of thousands of burned over acres of land that used to be forested that needs to be replanted. We have public parks and wilderness environments that need tending. We have camp grounds and public facilities that need constructing and maintaining. We have thousands of miles of streams that need cleaning. Most of this work is hard work and must be done by hand labor.

The government has been collected federal fuel taxes for decades. These taxes were to be used to maintain the roads and byways that the users paid them for. Like many other taxes collected for a purpose, these highway funds have been used for other pet projects of the politicians. Stolen, just like social security.

We have thousands of Bridges, dams, roads and public facilities that are in dire need of repair and maintenance. Some are to the point of being a danger to the public. We have actually had bridges collapse from lack of maintenance and kill people in the process.

America built hundreds of schools, medical clinics, bridges, and roads in Iraq and Afghanistan. America's needs have gone unmet while our politicians have given away our tax dollars and resources to countries that hate us.

Imagine, if America was to have an "Energy Boom" with several hundred drill rigs developing America's energy, the amount of taxes generated could fund the needed upgrading and repairs on America's infrastructure. Think of the thousands of jobs this would create.

Wake up Americans you are getting screwed by your government. Ask your congress why or how they can build these hundreds of medical clinics, schools, miles of road and bridges in foreign countries while America is taking second place.

If you don't register and vote these people out of office they will continue to ruin America.

CHAPTER #18
AMERICA'S ENERGY CRISIS

America currently imports the majority of its energy needs in the form of crude oil. There are alternatives to this drain on our economy to foreign governments. Our American energy reserves could supply our needs and possibly export some energy. Until our form of government is updated, congress will remain bought and paid for. The major oil companies have too much invested in foreign oil and gas fields where the operating rules and tax structures are far easier than in America. Again the American people have taken second or third place in congressional priorities.

Alaska has more than 30 trillion cubic feet of proven natural gas reserves with less than 5% of the area explored. Another 160 trillion cubic feet is thought to exist. Northern Canada has many trillions of cubic feet of natural gas in the Canadian Arctic and only a small area explored so far. The contiguous 48 states have proven reserves in the trillions of cubic feet of natural gas and natural gas Liquids.

Alaska has billions of barrels of oil and gas forever locked up. It was locked up by the order of Jimmy Carter when he had his one term presidency. In my opinion locking up Alaska against the Alaskan's wishes was a traitorous and criminal act that should have been immediately undone by his successor president. I have seen numerous televised congressional hearing to open parts of Alaska for energy extraction. The liberals continue to resist by any means possible be it foul, illegal or immoral. Rightly put, they lie like hell to keep Alaska locked up forever.

About 84 trillion cubic feet of undiscovered, technically recoverable gas lie in the Marcellus Shale under New York and seven other states. U.S. Geological Survey said Aug. 23, 2011.

The "Bakken" deposit found by the USGS is one of the largest deposits of oil and gas ever found in the contiguous 48 states. The "Bakken" underlay's three states and parts of southern Canada. The edges of the discovery still have not been accurately determined. The estimates vary but all of them agree that the reserves are in the multibillions in oil, natural gas and natural gas liquids. Development of this discovery would seriously curtail our foreign energy imports and could well make us energy independent on foreign oil.

The development of these two discoveries would create hundreds of thousands of direct jobs for Americans by private industry instead being paid for by taxpayers.

Imagine several hundred light drill rigs developing these American Resources would provide thousands of direct employment plus the support services these drill rigs would need. The tubular goods, materials, and consumables used is an industry in itself. The building of new light drill rigs to develop America's energy reserves would create hundreds of thousands of direct employment. Building the pipeline grid to distribute America's own natural gas would create thousands of high paying jobs. The servicing and maintenance of this system would provide thousands of jobs. The hundreds of billions of dollars flowing out of America to foreign countries would stop and that money would be spent here in America.

Americans using more natural gas would reduce our green house gas emissions. Hundreds of thousands of new jobs would be created and America could be on the way to energy independence.

The economic multiplier effect in our economy would create millions more jobs. More important, it would go a long ways toward a balance of trade.

Natural gas provides feed stock for the petrochemical industry, heat for homes and industry. Natural gas can be made into clean burning methanol (CH_3OH) to run our cars. Natural gas provides the fertilizers that make the American Farmer the envy of the world. Utilizing our natural gas supply and oil reserves to their full potential would create millions of new American jobs. The reduction in air pollution would a major step toward stopping or slowing down global warming.

A tenfold increase in the use of natural gas would save the hundreds of billions of dollars from going to foreign governments and create hundreds of thousands of direct high paying American jobs. With the financial multiplier effect of this action, again millions more of jobs would be created indirectly.

Most of the current hydrocarbon production areas require a procedure known as "Fracturing". In fracturing, producers force chemically treated water and proppants into underground shale wells to break up rock and let gas and oil flow easier. The U.S. Environmental Protection Agency is studying the effects of fracturing because opponents say it's a threat to drinking water. Fracturing hydrocarbon bearing formations improves the production and extends the production life of a well or field. Properly done, fracturing is a safe procedure. The fracturing industry employs thousands of people with high paying jobs.

America's vast proven natural gas reserves are enough to replace most of our crude oil imports. In my opinion, the major petroleum producers are part of the lobbying crew that owns the congress. As long as the U.S Congress remains in its current configuration, America's oil and natural gas will remain in the ground. The drain of currency out of America to foreigners will continue. Our unemployed Americans won't be able to develop our energy independence in our own country.

You can wager safely that the environmentalists will line up to stop all of the American oil and gas production that they can by any means fair or foul. In one sense, I can partially agree with environmental folks.

The oil companies need close, strict and comprehensive safety and compliance monitoring by professionals that thoroughly understand the petroleum industry. But, having said that, the creation of millions of high paying jobs, for Americans would far outweigh any environmental concerns, with little or no risk to our environment.

The potential production of energy in America could eliminate unemployment and keep hundreds of Billions of dollars in America. Since we have the best congress that money can buy, our American Energy Reserves will stay in the ground and the millions of jobs the development would create will never happen. Wake up American Voters, you being screwed..

It is past time to update and modernize our form of government. Americans get involved and vote out the scoundrels that are bankrupting America. It is time for the "Responsible Party". Americans, think about it , a political body that is not full of amoral career politicians. A congress that again has its citizen legislators as our founding fathers envisioned. Our legislators need to care more about the rank and file of American citizens, than they do of the amoral people that are in control of Washington D.C.

The change to a unicameral congress will go a long way to solving the problem.

Chapter #19
The Health Care Crisis

The solution to the health care crisis is fairly simple. America needs to implement a "single payer system". This system would be self funding and would bring the much needed competition to help solve the problems in the health care industry. The current health care industry, so far, has adamantly opposed a "Single Payer System".

To date, the U.S. Congress has declined to hear testimony on the single payer system. A single payer system has been the constant fear of the current health care industry who doesn't want any options for the American consumer. The health care lobby is one of the largest in our Capital, so I doubt there will be any meaningful change in the foreseeable future.

With careful management and planning the current "Medicare" organization could be formed into the single payer system. The transformation would need to include investigation and prosecution of the current fraud plaguing Medicare. If the U.S. Congress were to be forced to use Medicare as their medical benefit, as proposed elsewhere in this book, I think the transformation would come pretty quickly. Currently it takes one year to get on Medicare after the need is established. Many of the people who needed Medicare when they first qualified have died waiting the year for benefits. Medicare should have originally paid 95% of benefits instead of the miserly 80% it currently pays. Medicare should have included the following from the start:

- General and special health care
- Prescription drugs.
- Dental care.
- Mental health.
- Optical benefits.
-

These benefits would have made Medicare comparable to what the Congress voted them for health care coverage with money stolen from the social security trust fund...

"The institute of Medicine back in 2002 concluded that about 18,000 Americans die every year because of lack of health insurance". The U.S. Congress should be ashamed of this record. You spend billions of dollars on pet pork projects and giving money away to foreign countries while American citizens are dying from lack of medical care.

In 1986, Congress enacted the Emergency Medical Treatment & Labor Act (EMTALA) to ensure public access to emergency services regardless of ability to pay. Section 1867 of the Social Security Act imposes specific obligations on Medicare-participating hospitals that offer emergency services to provide a medical screening examination (MSE) when a request is made for examination or treatment for an emergency medical condition (EMC), including active labor, regardless of an individual's ability to pay.

Hospitals are then required to provide stabilizing treatment for patients with EMCs. If a hospital is unable to stabilize a patient within its capability, or if the patient requests, an appropriate transfer should be implemented.

This unfunded federal mandate has been one of the main contributing factors to our spiraling health care costs. When a medical facility is forced to take in patients that the facility has no hope of collecting money from, the rest of us have to pay for that medical care by increased cost in for our health care and healthcare insurance.

The EMTALA Act has driven up health care costs almost beyond the reach of average working American Citizens. The act has bankrupted numerous hospitals and medical services. There is no end in sight to this debacle. The number of illegal aliens that are swamping our medical care facilities will continue to increase. In my opinion, because our cowardly and incompetent congress won't act on the problem.

Illegal aliens are provided better health care than most Americans because of the "EMTALA Act".

I say to the congress it is time to repeal the EMTALA Act, and stop passing unfunded mandates on the American People. In my opinion, congress is too cowardly and irresponsible to act on this injustice, they get too many votes from these low life's that are ruining our healthcare systems.

For further reading on the obscene cost of illegal aliens go to;
"The American Surgeons and Physicians Journal Volume 10 #1 spring 2005"

Read the Article by Madeleine Pelner Cosman.

She has the credentials that give this article high credibility. The American healthcare industry is being swamped with illegal lowlifes.

For God's Sake Americans register and vote and get involved in saving America!

CHAPTER #20
THE GLOBAL WARMING CRISIS

I spent many years in Alaska working in the deep Arctic at Prudhoe Bay and across the North Slope. I started there in 1977 helping to put some of the first oil down the Trans-Alaska Pipeline. When I started there, the winter work season for construction when the tundra was frozen and we could work on it without harming it was mid October through mid March. In 2010 the work season had shortened up to barely ten weeks from late November to mid February. That tells me that some of the claims about global warming coming from the environmental community are valid.

What can Americans do about global warming? First, start using our natural abundant natural gas reserves for our energy needs and stop importing so much foreign oil. Natural gas can heat our homes, power our industry, fuel our vehicles both personal and commercial, and provide feed stock for many of our chemical industries. Natural gas is cleaner burning than coal or oil and emits much less harmful discharge into our atmosphere.

Americans need to take global warming seriously. The results if the warming continues will be catastrophic to say the least.

The development of America's natural gas resources coupled with the ingenuity of the American Auto Manufacturers would go a long ways to cutting down on the green house gases currently generated.

I carefully read Al Gore's book on global warming and some of it is, in my opinion, valid. Some of it is less than true.

The fact of the matter is that Americans are going to continue to drive up and down our highways freighting goods and transporting people for business and pleasure. What they need to do is use a cleaner fuel and more efficient vehicles.

CHAPTER #21
PICKING THE PEOPLE
TO SERVE AMERICA

With the two party system, the selection of the candidates to represent you in a unicameral congress are going to be made for you with little or no input from you the American voter.

I believe that all candidates should be drug tested and have background checks before being allowed to serve. Drug use, domestic violence, bankruptcy, fraud, or substance abuse is just some of the disqualifying things that should be enforced. Again, where in hell are the investigative reporters?

Thought should be given by the American Voters on how they pick their representation in a unicameral legislature. One of the problems facing that choice is often those who are best qualified and the most capable refuse to have anything to do with political office. When a unicameral legislature comes into being with the strict term limits proposed, I believe that with the elimination of career politicians, that some of our business leaders and managers would view their obligation to our country differently.

Until we can convince our brightest business leaders to run for congress instead of buying it, we will continue with our broken government as it is today. We need to draft these leaders, as Lee Iacocca suggests, with the best interests of American Voters at heart. With an eight year term limit and a unicameral congress the change in our government would be mind boggling. Balanced budgets, illegal immigrants deported, borders secured, less taxes, integrity back in our government, the list is endless.

What Americans need to understand is that if you don't register and vote responsibly, our country will be gone as we know it in this next generation. I hear many people say that their one vote won't make a difference. But I see elections with less than 50% voter turnout and I am saddened that the American people do not have a higher value on their freedom and way of life. The non-voters are allowing the politicians to steal their freedom and liberty from them and their descendants.

I suggest that you read Lee Iacocca's book, "Where have all the leaders gone".

Chapter #22
The Housing and
Real Estate Crisis.

When the housing boom got going full swing about 2005, the real estate brokers nationwide were having a field day. It was a seller's market and houses were selling at full price and people were selling and trading up and first time home buyers were bidding against each other over houses. Then came the "NINJA Loans" (no income no job or assets). These loans were packaged and sold to the big finance institutions with very little oversight. Many of these loans were to illegal immigrants and subsequently purchased in packages sold to the two federal government agencies, Freddie Mac and Fannie Mae. I am not convinced that with all the degrees, "MBA's, CPA's PhD's, JD's" etc; that the financial industry did not know the true value of the paper that was being packaged and sold. Your tax dollars at work again for illegal aliens.

Then, came the financial "meltdown" of the finance and housing industry. There had been very little oversight by the government agencies up to the point of the crisis thanks to many high dollar campaign contributions to Washington D.C. Politicians

The resulting TARP (toxic asset relief program) paper ended up being paid for by the American Taxpayers. The huge financial "Bailouts" were your tax dollars saving the financial industry from itself. The purchase of congress turned out to be a bargain for them. They got saved by the taxpayers and got to keep all their personal wealth that rightfully belonged to their shareholders.

Several of the finance people partially responsible for the financial mess were active on Obama's campaign. Fund raising, managing campaign funds, helping select a vice-presidential candidate.

The managers of the financial industry that were responsible for the debacle have taken their obscene bonuses and have stayed low profile. In my opinion, most of them should have had their fortunes stripped from them and sent to jail just like Bernie Madoff was. Somehow, I don't think that will happen. In my opinion, they own the politicians in Washington bought and paid for.

Bernie Madoff's "PONZI" scheme was revealed to SEC years before it was acknowledged by law enforcement by some very reliable sources. The SEC took no action to investigate the information for several years. I wonder who was paying who off and with what?

Many of the financial industry people still collected their obscene" merit bonuses", "retention bonuses", etc; even though they were running a publicly traded company into bankruptcy.

In my opinion these people belong in prison right alongside of Bernie Madoff.

But somehow I think our current president and, in my opinion, his incompetent attorney general are not going to do anything to hold these people accountable for what they did to the American finance industry.

Here again, your tax dollars at work, in a bought and paid for congress.

Chapter #23
The American Penal System

Here is an example of how our penal system could be improved.

Used with consent.

SHERIFF JOE IS AT IT AGAIN!
You all remember Sheriff Joe Arpaio of Arizona, who painted the jail cells pink and made the inmates wear pink prison garb. Well.........

Oh, there's MUCH more to know about Sheriff Joe!

Maricopa County was spending approx. $18 million dollars a year on stray animals, like cats and dogs. Sheriff Joe offered to take the department over and the County Supervisors said okay.

The animal shelters are now all staffed and operated by prisoners. They feed and care for the strays. Every animal in his care is taken out and walked twice daily. He now has prisoners who are experts in animal nutrition and behavior. They give great classes for anyone who'd like to adopt an animal. He has literally taken stray dogs off the street, given them to the care of prisoners, and had them place in dog shows.

The best part? His budget for the entire department is now under $3 million. An adopted a Weimaraner from a Maricopa County shelter two years ago had been neutered and was current on all shots, in great health, and even had a microchip inserted the day he was adopted. The cost for the adoption $78.

The prisoners get the benefit of about $0.28 an hour for working, but most would work for free, just to be out of their cells for the day. Most of his budget is for utilities, building maintenance, etc. He pays the prisoners out of the fees collected for adopted animals.

I have long wondered when the rest of the country would take a look at the way he runs the jail system and copy some of his ideas. He has a huge farm, donated to the county years ago, where inmates can work, and they grow most of their own fresh vegetables and food, doing all the work and harvesting by hand.

He has a pretty good sized hog farm, which provides meat and fertilizer. It fertilizes the Christmas tree nursery, where prisoners work, and you can buy a living Christmas tree for $6 - $8 for the holidays and plant it later. Many Arizona Residents have several trees in their yard from prior Christmas'.

Yup, he was re-elected last year with 83% of the vote.

Now he's in trouble with the ACLU again. He painted all his buses and vehicles with a mural that has a special hotline phone number painted on it, where you can call and report suspected illegal aliens. Immigrations and Customs Enforcement wasn't doing enough in his eyes, so he had 40 deputies trained specifically for enforcing immigration laws, started up his hotline, and bought 4 new buses just for hauling folks back to the border. He's kind of a 'Git-R Dun' kind of Sheriff.

TO THOSE OF YOU NOT FAMILIAR WITH JOE ARPAIO...

HE IS THE MARICOPA ARIZONA COUNTY SHERIFF

AND HE KEEPS GETTING ELECTED OVER AND OVER.

THIS IS ONE OF THE REASONS WHY:

- Sheriff Joe Arpaio (in Arizona) who created the 'Tent City Jail':
- **He has jail meals down to 40 cents a serving and charges the inmates for them.
- **He stopped smoking and porno magazines in the jails. **Took away their weights.
- **Cut off all but 'G' movies.
- **He started chain gangs so the inmates could do free work on county and city projects.
- **Then he started chain gangs for women so he wouldn't get sued for discrimination.
- **He took away cable TV until he found out there was a federal court order that required cable TV for jails, so he hooked up the cable TV again.....BUT only let in the Disney channel and the Weather channel.
- **When asked why the weather channel, he replied, "So they will know how hot it's going to be while they are working on my chain gangs."

- **He cut off coffee since it has zero nutritional value.
- **When the inmates complained, he told them, "This isn't The Ritz/Carlton...... If you don't like it, don't come back."

More On The Arizona Sheriff:

With temperatures being even hotter than usual in Phoenix (116 degrees just set a new record), the Associated Press reports:

About 2,000 inmates living in a barbed-wire-surrounded tent encampment at the Maricopa County jail have been given permission to strip down to their government-issued pink boxer shorts.

On Wednesday, hundreds of men wearing boxers were either curled up on their bunk beds or chatted in the tents, which reached 138 degrees inside the week before.

Many were also swathed in wet, pink towels as sweat collected on their chests and dripped down to their PINK SOCKS.

"It feels like we are in a furnace," said an inmate who has lived in the TENTS for 1 year. "It's inhumane."

Joe Arpaio, the tough-guy sheriff who created the tent city and long ago started making his prisoners wear pink and eat bologna sandwiches, is not one bit sympathetic. He said Wednesday that he told all of the inmates, "its 120 degrees in Iraq and our soldiers are living in tents too, and they have to wear full battle gear, but they didn't commit any crimes, so shut your mouths!"

Way to go, Sheriff!

Maybe if all prisons were like this one there would be a lot less crime and/or repeat offenders. Criminals should be punished for their crimes - not live in luxury until it's time for their parole, only to go out and commit another crime so they can get back in to live on taxpayers' money and enjoy things taxpayers can't afford to have for themselves.

The State of Colorado is using inmates to care for, train and help with the adoption of captured wild horses. The captured horses are trained and taken care of by state inmates instead of going to the slaughter house. The inmates receive a small wage and the program is self-funding from the sale of the trained horses to the public.

The State of California has for many years operated conservation camps for the training and rehabilitation of minimum security inmates. The inmates live in open camps at numerous locations around California and are trained in fire suppression and other public emergencies. The rate of recidivism from the camp programs in significantly less than the rest of the maximum security facilities. This inmate program has been responsible for building and maintaining public campgrounds and other public service property. The reforestation program has planted millions of trees on fire damaged public land.

My question to the correction industry is why are not all of the minimum security inmates being utilized for public projects that are not otherwise going to get done? Projects that are too expensive to hire private industry for that would not otherwise get done.

Millions of acres of public land need cleanup and reforestation. Thousands of miles of our national waterways need erosion control actions taken. These public benefits do not interfere with private industry. Most of the work done by current inmate work programs is work that is too expensive or difficult for private industry. Putting inmates to work is not cruel or unusual punishment. If an inmate work program was initiated, and the opportunity for earning sentence reduction for good behavior, hard work and getting an education, I would venture a guess that most inmates would jump at the chance. Many of the work programs in the various penal systems have one thing in common. The programs are proven to reduce recidivism (repeat offenders) substantially.

Maybe the liberals should keep their damn noses out of such a program.

In my opinion, the death penalty has not been used enough. There are several crimes that I would support the death penalty to be applied.

Here is a partial list;

- The sale of illegal drugs to minor children
- Acts of terror against America.
- Murder of a Peace Officer.
- Premeditated murder.
- Drunk driving resulting in death.
- Smuggling illegal aliens into America
- High treason against America.

There have been numerous studies on the effect of capital Punishment. The liberals have resisted the application saying that life imprisonment is deterrent enough. Life imprisonment is an enormous cost to the tax payers. In my opinion, capital punishment might not be a deterrent, but it certainly stops repeat offenders.

CHAPTER # 24
RIGHT ON LEE IACOCCA

Remember Lee Iacocca, the man who rescued Chrysler Corporation from its death throes? He's now passed 82 years old and has a new book, and here are some excerpts used with the Consent of Lee Iacocca.

Lee Iacocca Says:

"Am I the only guy in this country who's fed up with what's happening? Where the hell is our outrage? We should be screaming bloody murder. We've got a gang of clueless bozos steering our ship of state right over a cliff, we've got corporate gangsters stealing us blind, and we can't even clean up after a hurricane much less build a hybrid car. But instead of getting mad, everyone sits around and nods their heads when the politicians say, "Stay the course"

Stay the course? You've got to be kidding. This is America, not the damned "Titanic". I'll give you a sound bite: "Throw all the bums out!"

You might think I'm getting senile, that I've gone off my rocker, and maybe I have. But someone has to speak up. I hardly recognize this country anymore.

The most famous business leaders are not the innovators but the guys in handcuffs. While we're fiddling in Iraq, the Middle East is burning and nobody seems to know what to do. And the press is waving 'pom -poms' instead of asking hard questions. That's not the promise of the " America" my parents and yours traveled across the ocean for. I've had enough. How about you?

I'll go a step further. You can't call yourself a patriot if you're not outraged. This is a fight I'm ready and willing to have. The Biggest "C" is Crisis! (Iacocca elaborates on nine Cs of leadership, crisis being the first.)

Leaders are made, not born. Leadership is forged in times of crisis. It's easy to sit there with your feet up on the desk and talk theory. Or send someone else's kids off to war when you've never seen a battlefield yourself. It's another thing to lead when your world comes tumbling down.

On September 11, 2001, we needed a strong leader more than any other time in our history. We needed a steady hand to guide us out of the ashes. A Hell of a Mess So here's where we stand. We're immersed in a bloody war with no plan for winning and no plan for leaving. We're running the biggest deficit in the history of the country. We're losing the manufacturing edge to Asia, while our once-great companies are getting slaughtered by health care costs. Gas prices are skyrocketing, and nobody in power has a coherent energy policy. Our schools are in trouble. Our borders are like sieves. The middle class is being squeezed every which way these are times that cry out for leadership.

But when you look around, you've got to ask:" Where have all the leaders gone?" Where are the curious, creative communicators? Where are the people of character, courage, conviction, omnipotence, and common sense? I may be a sucker for alliteration, but I think you get the point.

Name me a leader who has a better idea for homeland security than making us take off our shoes in airports and throw away our shampoo? We've spent billions of dollars building a huge new bureaucracy, and all we know how to do is react to things that have already happened.

Name me one leader who emerged from the crisis of Hurricane Katrina. Congress has yet to spend a single day evaluating the response to the hurricane, or demanding accountability for the decisions that were made in the crucial hours after the storm.

Everyone's hunkering down, fingers crossed, hoping it doesn't happen again. Now, that's just crazy. Storms happen. Deal with it. Make a plan. Figure out what you're going to do the next time.

Name me an industry leader who is thinking creatively about how we can restore our competitive edge in manufacturing. Who would have believed that there could ever be a time when "The Big Three" referred to Japanese car companies? How did this happen, and more important, what are we going to do about it?

Name me a government leader who can articulate a plan for paying down the debit, or solving the energy crisis, or managing the health care problem.

The silence is deafening. But these are the crises that are eating away at our country and milking the middle class dry.

I have news for the gang in Congress. We didn't elect you to sit on your asses

And do nothing and remain silent while our democracy is being hijacked and our greatness is being replaced with mediocrity. What is everybody so afraid of?

That some bonehead on Fox News will call them a name? Give me a break. Why don't you guys show some spine for a change?

Had Enough?

Hey, I'm not trying to be the voice of gloom and doom here. I'm trying to light a fire. I'm speaking out because I have hope I believe in America. In my lifetime I've had the privilege of living through some of America's greatest moments. I've also experienced some of our

Worst crises: the "Great Depression", "World War II", the "Korean War",

The "Kennedy Assassination", the "Vietnam War", the 1970's oil crisis,

And the struggles of recent years culminating with 9/11. If I've learned one thing, it's this:

"You don't get anywhere by standing on the sidelines waiting for somebody else to take action. Whether it's building a better car or building a better future for our children, we all have a role to play.

That's the challenge I'm raising in this book. It's a call to "Action"

For people who, like me, believe in America.

It's not too late, but it's getting pretty close. So let's shake off the crap

And go to work. Let's tell 'em all we've had "enough."

Make your own contribution by encouraging everyone you know and care about to get involved with you in taking back this country. It's our country, folks; and it's our future. Our future is at stake!

I have admired Lee Iacocca for many years. He is, in my opinion, a Great American and he should have been President, America needed him.

Chapter #25
The right to bear arms
The 2nd Amendment

1. "Those who hammer their guns into plows will plow for those who do not." ~Thomas Jefferson
2. Those that trade liberty for security have neither. ~John Adams
3. Free men do not ask permission to bear arms.
4. An armed man is a citizen. An unarmed man is a subject.
5. Only a government that is afraid of its citizens tries to dis-arm them.
6. Gun control is not about guns; it's about control.
7. You only have the rights you are willing to fight for.
8. No guns, know peace, know safety. No guns, no peace, no safety.
9. You don't shoot to kill; you shoot to stay alive.
10. Assault is a behavior, not a device.
11. 64,999,987 firearms owners killed no one yesterday.

12. The United States Constitution (c) 1791. All Rights Reserved.
13. 1The Second Amendment is in place in case the politicians ignore the others.
14. What part of 'shall not be infringed' do you NOT understand?
15. Guns have only two enemies; rust and politicians.
16. When you remove the people's right to bear arms, you create slaves.
17. The American Revolution would never have happened with gun control.

I believe that there should be a federal law protecting the right to defend yourself and your loved ones. If a home intrusion happens and you shoot a criminal intruder or you are defending against a violent crime, you should be exempted by law from ANY liability civil or criminal.

The National Rifle Association has done a Marvelous job of promoting firearms safety and education. They have lobbied the congress countless hours and defended the 2nd Amendment admirably. The American People owe the N.R.A. a huge debt of thanks for their protection of our right to keep and bear arms. Without the NRA, we would have lost our rights to bear arms years ago. I hope Americans will say a prayer for the NRA and their un-daunting fight to protect our right to bear arms. Their continuing effort deserves the support all Americans.

The liberals will continue to try to take away ALL of Americans guns. The best way to stop this outrage is to get involved in choosing our political leaders, the only way to do that is to register and vote.

As I am writing this book, I received a letter from Senator Paul Rand (Rep Kentucky) About the liberals in Congress trying to get America to sign on to the "U.N. Small Arms Treaty" This treaty is ultimately intended to confiscate ALL fire arms in private citizens' possession worldwide. I do not see how the U.S. Senate can ratify a treaty that would violate the U.S. Constitution. But them the government seems adept at ignoring the constitution pretty often whenever in pleases them.

CHAPTER #26
GOVERNMENT WASTE

This article on government waste by the government accounting office starts to tell the tale much better than I can. I believe that these examples are just the tip off of a financial iceberg on government waste. As you read this public report, ask yourself why hasn't the media screamed loud and long about this huge amount of waste of the American Taxpayer's money? In my opinion, Most of our media both print and electronic are more interested in making news instead of responsibly reporting. I say to the American media that you can help save America by bringing conduct like described here to the attention of the American Voters.

The politicians steal our money with the help and cooperation of the I.R.S. and this is what they do with it among other wastes. But their cohort, the I.R.S., is right there to make sure that the politicians have plenty of our money to spend.

This article is cited with "IWatch" consent

Published on **iWatch News** (http://www.iwatchnews.org)
Home > GAO cites billions of dollars in duplication, from military to highways

Accountability [1]

GAO cites billions of dollars in duplication, from military to highways [2]

It is one of the inexplicable facets of government: Duplication across agencies and departments at a cost of billions of dollars to taxpayers.

One example: Attempts to develop safety measures against improvised explosive devices has seen two parallel groups in the Marine and Army developing their own technologies. Congress has approved $17 billion for IED research. The Army has a mine roller costing $77,000 to $225,000 per unit. The Marines have built similar anti-IED equipment for $85,000. There is still disagreement on which one works better.

GAO, the watchdog arm of the federal government, has weighed in with a series of suggestions with the potential to save taxpayers billions of dollars simply by eliminating duplicated efforts by government agencies

"GAO has identified a mother lode of government waste and duplication that should keep Congress busy for the rest of the year," Sen. Tom Coburn of R-Okla. said.

Covering over 30 areas of government spending where program overlap has led to "unnecessary duplication" the report finds that "reducing or eliminating duplication, overlap or fragmentation could potentially save billions of taxpayer dollars annually and help agencies provide more efficient and effective services." The first of what is slated to be an annual series on duplication in government; the report was directed by an amendment from Sen. Coburn during last year's vote on the debt limit.

In some cases the GAO discovered that "financial benefits ranging from the tens of millions to several billion dollars annually may be realized by addressing that single issue," with the report specifically citing the Department of Defense's military health care system, where "broader restructuring could result in annual savings of up to $460 million."

Other areas of duplication:

The conflict between various branches of law enforcement, such as the Federal Bureau of Investigation and the Bureau of Alcohol, Tobacco, Firearms and Explosives, over jurisdiction of investigations involving explosives. Coburn's office estimated there was $35 million spent in duplicated efforts related to the issue in fiscal year 2010.

In programs to aid the poor, Coburn's office estimated that $2.9 billion was spent in fiscal year 2009 on duplicated efforts among 20 programs to aid to the nation's homeless population. It also cited $62.5 billion in food assistance programs, spread across 18 programs in three federal departments.

Highways, a bane to every road warrior in the nation, are criticized for being governed by more than 100 separate programs. "The current approach to surface transportation was established in 1956 to build the Interstate Highway System but has not evolved to reflect current priorities in transportation planning," the report said. Even as the government strives to reduce its reliance on fossil fuels for the federal fleet, the report noted the feds spent $1.9 billion in new vehicles in fiscal 2009 and gassed up the existing fleet of 600,000 vehicles to the tune of 963,000 gallons of fuel per day.

The report "shows we could save taxpayers hundreds of billions of dollars every year without cutting services," Coburn said in a statement.

Entitled "Opportunities to Reduce Potential Duplication in Government Programs, Save Tax Dollars, and Enhance Revenue," the report is now available [3] on the GAO's website.

Featured title:

It is one of the inexplicable facets of government: duplication across agencies

It is one of the inexplicable facets of government: duplication across agencies and departments at a cost of billions of dollars to taxpayer

---

Source URL: http://www.iwatchnews.org/2011/03/01/2106/gao-cites-billions-dollars-duplication-military-highways

This is not the only group that has documented government waste and duplication of services. The bureaucrats that run these agencies will stop at nothing to save and preserve their publicly funded kingdoms.

The regulatory agencies are beyond and decent control. Medical breakthroughs that could have saved a multitude of lives takes years and millions of dollars to fight the way through Federal Drug Administration. In my opinion, these delays and endless hearings are bordering on criminal conduct by the folks that are in conflict with personal interests.

Resource extraction permits take years for approval with the liberal environmentalists' fighting them every step of the way. The classic example is "ANWR" (arctic national wildlife refuge) locked up by an ignorant president and defended by liberal environmentalists'. "ANWR" is a desolate mosquito infested nightmare in the summer and a frozen desolate hell in the winter. But to hear the liberals resist development you would think it was an Eden on earth. They lie, cheat, mislead and perjure themselves for their cause.

The President of the United States has to be the one to stop these publicly funded kingdoms. The president must issue presidential orders closing the duplicated services and get rid of these public parasites. So far no president elected has had the courage to clean house in Washington D.C.

I wonder if any of the 2012 Candidates have the guts to clean up this unholy mess?

CHAPTER #27
FOREIGN AID THE
POLITICAL GIVE-A-AWAY

Every year American Politicians send billions of dollars of American Taxpayer's dollars to foreign countries. Egypt, Pakistan, Saudi Arabia, etc; Many of the countries that the politicians send foreign aid to have factions that hate America and will do anything they can to hurt or destroy our American way of life.

I can understand helping people that are starving and in dire need. But much of the foreign aid has been for military support and arms in countries where the people are living at or below the starvation point.

Our American Farmers are the envy of the world and are capable of feeding the starving people all over the world. In fact, our farmers are so successful that our government pays some of them subsidies to not grow food. Go figure.

We have impoverished people right here in America, but I see resources being sent foreign countries and our Americans in need being ignored. America has people that live at or below the poverty line while our politicians send your tax dollars out of the country to people that hate America. Every night in

America there are people, adults and children living in poverty and going to bed hungry. U.S. Congress hang your head in shame!

Africa, Latin America, Southeast Asia, the sub continent, all have people in dire need.

In some countries the infant mortality approaches 30%. In some countries many people are born and live their whole lives without ever a visit to a doctor or dentist. I can see helping people in need when America can spare the resources. But maybe the politicians should take a look at home first.

There is no reason for any Americans to be homeless or in need. The fact that some American children go to bed hungry every night is a national shame. The fact that we have American veterans going without needed help that they were promised is a national shame on the politicians. One of our Senators sent $20,000,000.00 dollars to a foreign country to help with clothes for their military. The 20 million dollars disappeared and the soldiers were still naked and barefoot.

My question to the media is why in the hell are you not reporting this to the American People? With some notable exceptions, in my opinion our American media both print and electronic are craven irresponsible cowards that are basking in the limelight of being themselves and their notoriety instead of telling the American People just how bad their Government is giving them the shaft.

CHAPTER #28
OUR ENVIRONMENTAL CRISIS

We are becoming a disposable society. Americans take for granted that there always be more or a replacement. Every week when I haul our household waste to the transfer station, I see people throwing away containers with a cash deposit value. I cannot speak for the rest of America but I would not walk past a nickel lying on the ground because it wasn't enough to pick up.

I would be in favor of placing a $1.00 deposit on all drink containers. Maybe American would think twice about throwing away $1.00 as opposed to $.05.

There would certainly be more people picking up the throw-away's for the $1.00 deposit.

I walk by dumpsters and see used furniture, tools, household items, yard items, which are mostly repairable just thrown away because they were out of style and somebody bought a new and better one.

I plant a large vegetable garden every summer and my family enjoys fresh produce until the fall frost. I have asked many people with room to plant a vegetable garden why they didn't plant something. The answer was "it was too much trouble or it's too much work".

Our atmosphere is being polluted by burning too many fossil fuels like coal when America has trillions of cubic feet of clean burning natural gas reserves. You can wager with fair certainty that the environmentalists will line up to stop any development of America's natural gas reserves

I see people buying bottled water at some ridiculous price and just throwing the bottle away. The Television ads tell me that there enough water bottles sold every year to circle the earth several times if placed end to end. I wonder how many of those bottles would be recycled if there were to be $1.00 federal cash deposit on them?

I do not agree entirely with Al Gore in his book but I believe that we are entering a warming period that will have profound effects on America in the not distant future if we do not take action.

CHAPTER #29
VOTER REGISTRATION
AND VOTING

In my opinion, I believe that the democrats have registered as many of the illegal aliens that they were able to. Without the low class vote of the illegal's and welfare recipients, the democrats would have a hard time winning any election. In my opinion, the democrats with their initial theft of the Social Security Trust Fund to the numerous give away programs they have sponsored over the years, they cannot win an election where the American Taxpayers are the majority voters. Keeping that opinion in mind, consider this analysis of the last election.

Searching the 2010 census records and the federal election records, results in some interesting Facts.

Number of States won by: Obama: 19
    McCain: 29
Square miles of land won by:
    Obama: 580,000
    McCain: 2,427,000
Population of counties
    Won by: Obama: 127 million

McCain: 143 million
Murder rate per 100,000 residents in counties won by:
   Obama: 13.2
   McCain: 2.1

The map of the territory McCain won was mostly the land owned by the taxpaying citizens of the country.

Obama territory mostly encompassed those citizens living in low income areas and living off various forms of government entitlement programs.

If Congress grants amnesty and citizenship to twenty million criminal invaders called illegal's, and they vote, the we can say goodbye to the USA in fewer than five years.

If you are in favor of this, then by all means continue to not vote or get involved with electing our leaders. Americans must all realize just how much is at stake, knowing that apathy is the greatest danger to our freedom.

For god's sakes Americans get involved our country is being stolen from us and you are allowing it to happen!

CHAPTER #30
MY SYNOPSIS

As I wrote this book, I have hammered repeatedly on getting you involved and helping to take our America back from those people who are stealing it. The liberal politicians are using the illegal immigrants that are here in America for the free ride. The job won't be easy. The middle American Voters have delayed to long jumping into the fight to save America.

To save America as we know it, we must have a 98%+ voter turnout of the taxpaying Americans that are being ripped off by the government at every election. The huge silent majority of Middle America must go to the polls. Now the lowlifes that are on welfare and some of the illegals are turning out in droves to protect their free ride at the taxpayer's expense. We need to establish strong citizen identification at the polling places. Illegal Immigrants have no right to vote in our American Elections. But care must be taken to ensure that the requirement for identification does not become a dis-enfranchisement of the lawful voters

We need for our business leaders, our educators, and our common citizens to step forward and run for public office to contribute their knowledge and ability to set America back on the path our founding fathers envisioned for all Americans.

Washington D.C. and surrounding area has the lowest un-employment rate of America. The public parasites are rampant in our government. There numerous government agencies and bureaus that duplicate each other. Congress must put a stop to the patronage and streamline our government.

We need to follow the examples set by three of our previous presidents and start immediately deporting the illegal aliens that are dragging America down. Deport them by the bus loads, airplane loads and ship loads. Then we need to secure our borders and stop them from sneaking back in.

We need to empty our prisons and deport the convicts to their native country and if they sneak back into America, shoot them on sight.

We need to re-establish our Social Security Trust fund as we were originally promised and then place it beyond the reach of thieving politicians. The trust was stolen by the democrats and then spent by both the republicans and the democrats. Congress must be forced pay back to the people all the money they stole with interest. A board of directors should be established to manage the Social Security Trust Fund within full public view and accountable to the people who own the trust.

The 2012 presidential election is going to be dominated by the liberal media. Obama is their "poster boy" and they will give him all the help they can legal, amoral or otherwise to get him re-elected. So far, as I write this book, the republican candidates vying for 2012 are shooting themselves in the foot and everyone standing around them.

I watched the debate on November 5th, debate between Herman Cain and Newt Gingrich and if Newt Gingrich is telling the truth, he knows his way around the capital politics and might make a good president? Mitt Romney is the only true for profit business man that I see in the race. Maybe they will team up and work together? If they would reconcile their differences, they would be a formidable team for America in our nation's capital.

I pray every day that competent "responsible" candidates will appear on the scene. Jesse Ventura where are you? Notice, I wrote "responsible" not democrat or republican. Maybe if we are fortunate, some of our business leaders and educators will step forward and help Middle America start to take back our country.

In my opinion, it is past time for a Middle America third party to rise and take control of America.

The internet was invaluable in researching a lot of this book. The information contained can mostly be validated on the internet. I have cited the url in many places. I hope that some of the readers will take the initiative to search on the internet and help me spread the words to their friends and neighbors about the crisis that America is facing.